Narcissism

Clinical Insights Into Personality Disorders: Empowering Yourself In The Context Of Narcissistic Relationships

(The Delineations Of Psychology And Human Behaviors)

Houston Salazar

TABLE OF CONTENT

Methods For Detecting Narcissistic Traits 1

How Can You Leave That Toxic Relationship Even When You're Still In Love With Your Partner? 18

Self-Esteem Vs. Narcissism 39

Types Of Narcissists 60

Dealing With Vanity 78

Narcissistic Mother 101

Metallization-Based Therapy 115

Obsessive Creatures 146

How To Cope With The Challenges You Have Encountered 159

Methods For Detecting Narcissistic Traits

Have you ever been involved in a romantic relationship with someone who appears to have a strong and genuine interest in you? They lavish you with presents, perhaps whisk you away on opulent excursions, unexpectedly appear at your workplace with gifts—offering the full extent of their efforts. Yet, abruptly, without warning, it ceases entirely. They refrain from initiating contact with you or disregard your communication for a temporary period, utilizing busyness, work obligations, or familial affairs as justifications for their lack of engagement.

They display a sincere expression of remorse, subsequently returning to their deep level of engagement with you. The performance commences anew, accompanied by offerings, notable occasions, and affectionate gestures. Subsequently, we encounter a period characterized by total tranquility. What happened? Ladies and gentlemen, what we have here can be referred to as love bombing. The absence of communication from your partner elicits a sense of bewilderment within you. You initiate the action of engaging in self-doubt, which aligns with their anticipated expectation.

You find yourself contemplating if any mistakes were made on your part. Additionally, one may contemplate whether they are overreacting and commence rationalizing the conduct, as the individual they are romantically involved with exhibits a strong interest, leading them to attribute the issue to their own shortcomings. This statement lacks accuracy as it can be asserted that you are not the source of the problem. They are the problem. This individual is engaging in a recreational activity, as narcissistic individuals generally derive satisfaction from participating in games due to their inclination towards maintaining dominance and control. It can be considered a form of exerting dominance, whereby individuals derive pleasure from the realization of their significant influence over another person across various aspects.

If you have ever encountered the situation I have just portrayed, it is highly probable that you are engaging with an individual who exhibits narcissistic tendencies. Individuals who possess good mental and physical health, along with qualities such as empathy, love, and honesty, will abstain from engaging in this disruptive activity. On the contrary, they assume the responsibility of communicating with you by means of text messaging or telephone conversations. They do not abruptly cease communication and then reestablish contact after a lapse of four days. However, the narcissist's actions do not cease at that point. Sadly, there's more.

Have you ever observed your significant other engage in a particular behavior, only for them to outright deny it when you confront them about it? Have you ever encountered a scenario where individuals articulate something with utmost clarity, only to deny it when directly confronted? The act of denial is a conspicuous characteristic demonstrated by individuals with narcissistic tendencies. They will reject the validity of your perception. You perceive a sense of obligation to construct a compelling argument until the individuals in question acknowledge and assume accountability for their deeds, yet this acknowledgment perpetually eludes you. Adopting a strategy of denial is a preferred tactic for them, intended to ensure their own safety while perpetuating a cycle of confusion and evasion for you.

When individuals contemplate narcissism, the initial mental image that arises is that of conceit and egocentricity. Notwithstanding these surface characteristics exhibited by the narcissist, their profound behaviors extend far beyond the superficial realm. These include but are not limited to denial, gaslighting, love bombing, grandiosity, entitlement, control, as well as an absence of empathy and validation, among various other recurring patterns.

One of the most profound consequences of being in the company of a narcissist is the overwhelming feeling of inadequacy. One can ascertain that they are in a relationship with a narcissistic individual when they consistently undertake various responsibilities, such as upholding cleanliness within the household, engaging in physical exercise, maintaining a well-groomed appearance, preparing meals from scratch, and exceeding expectations. However, despite these efforts, their partner remains unresponsive or unreceptive, displaying neither a desire for personal growth nor expressing gratitude for their significant contributions. Thus, one can easily succumb to the misconception that by demonstrating greater affection towards them or adopting a more amiable demeanor, they will undergo a transformation.

This phenomenon can be likened to a fantasy inspired by the tale of Beauty and the Beast, in which one believes that by increasing their love for another, they can catalyze a transformation, causing them to evolve into the ideal affectionate, authentic, and perceptive partner one desires for oneself. Regrettably, it is merely an expression of hopeful speculation, as narcissism comprises a collection of ingrained behaviors that manifest in an individual from early childhood onwards. Narcissists are unaware of the necessity to enact any alteration in their behavior. Based on extensive research and the available literature, it can be concluded that their refusal and lack of willingness represent a futile allocation of resources.

Therefore, for individuals who are experiencing the effects of narcissism, it can be exasperating to shoulder all responsibilities and embody various roles, yet see no effect on the behavior of one's partner. The absence of empathy will have an impact on you. As individuals, we have an inherent inclination to express our thoughts and emotions and to be acknowledged and comprehended. However, there appears to be a lack of empathy towards the emotional distress, sorrow, or aggravation experienced by individuals in relationships with narcissistic partners. The narcissist will shift the blame onto you, distorting the truth in the process. They possess a high degree of proficiency in attributing responsibility and engendering within you a sense that you bear fault for all tumultuous circumstances within the relationship.

Narcissists are not born. They are raised. How so? The subsequent elements comprise the foundation for the manifestations of narcissistic behavior when combined. A child who has experienced parental neglect leading to unmet emotional needs during their formative years may be susceptible to developing narcissistic traits. A young individual who had to earn their parent's attention and affection by demonstrating academic excellence is currently acquiring the comprehension that love is a conditional acquisition rather than an inherent, unconditional emotion. Thus, you possess a prodigious individual who excels in a myriad of pursuits, including athletic endeavors. Externally, one may witness the presence of their parents on the bleachers, enthusiastically displaying their child's academic accomplishments and awards. However, regrettably, when the child is in dire need of emotional assistance, their parents are conspicuously absent. Put differently, it is subject to conditionality rather than unconditionality.

The emotional realm of a child remains unprotected and neglected. The depreciation of emotions fosters an element of shallowness within the fundamental essence of a child's existence and understanding of oneself. Therefore, engendering patterns of behavior characterized by the pursuit of validation, the seeking of attention, and the manifestation of grandiosity. Despite their outward displays of confidence, many narcissists are plagued by deep-seated feelings of insecurity and shame. Unbeknownst to them, they are earnestly pursuing validation from society, which explains their profound affinity for social media. Their need for validation is promptly fulfilled.

The absence of perception of their insecurity and shame can be attributed to their long-standing habit of concealing and suppressing their emotions. It appears as if they have undergone training that discourages their emotional expression. This may be extremely frustrating for the narcissist's partner, whose love language is an exchange of emotional connection.

Externally, a narcissist exudes charm and charisma. It is a component of their public image to conceal their emotional dysregulation, as well as other internal difficulties associated with emotions. They possess a captivating charm and effortlessly command attention, becoming the center of attention in any social setting.

Narcissism is not linear. In the upcoming chapter, we will explore an in-depth analysis of the four distinct categories encompassing the seven variations of narcissistic individuals. It is imperative to sustain our learning and pursuit of knowledge regarding this subject matter in order to ascertain these characteristics in individuals in close proximity or seeking a close relationship. Narcissistic conduct has the propensity to be predatory by effectively identifying vulnerability in others and exploiting it opportunistically. They possess a strong inclination towards competition and are willing to demean or degrade others in order to achieve success or advancement in fields such as business, professional endeavors, or various aspects of life. As we thoroughly examine the intricacies, we undertake this task in order to facilitate your comprehension of an individual who possesses these characteristics. Allow us to acquire the knowledge of effectively addressing individuals and relationships of this nature, thus protecting ourselves from emotional harm inflicted by such persons.

Grandiose Narcissism Traits

The initial characteristic of grandiose narcissists that warrants attention is their tendency to overinflate their positive attributes, particularly in regards to their cognitive aptitude. They have long been recognized for their inclination towards self-admiration, haughtiness, shallowness, preoccupation with authority, and, naturally, a sense of grandeur. They perceive themselves as being of higher status than individuals who possess an average measure of extraversion and openness. Given the inherent confidence narcissists possess in their capabilities and intellect, it is only natural for them to perceive themselves as more dominant than individuals who do not exhibit narcissistic tendencies. Grandiose narcissism is a characteristic that enables an individual to maintain a state of elation regardless of the presence or actions of those surrounding them. Individuals of this nature do not rely upon familial, friendly, or intimate connections for support. Although they may present themselves as affectionate partners or compassionate companions, their true intentions are merely to create a façade for public consumption. There is an apparent lack of genuine sincerity or true dedication towards their loved ones. The relationship consistently revolves solely around their individualistic needs and desires. Their reliance on another individual is always devoid of any emotional motives. It is evident that engaging in a normal, healthy relationship with individuals who possess grandiose narcissistic tendencies is not feasible, as they do not demonstrate the necessary willingness for mutual compromise and exchange.

The Personality Type of Grandiosity and its Relevance in Leadership Positions

A narcissist with grandiose tendencies may be well-suited for positions of leadership due to their exceptionally extroverted personality traits. Despite their lack of competency to secure a position or advance professionally, they persist in believing that they deserve it. In pursuit of heightened confidence and a sense of assurance, individuals possessing extroverted tendencies and grandiose traits endeavor to obtain the approval and benevolence of individuals who exhibit a disposition of apparent agreeableness and aversion to conflict. In the event that individuals do not receive commendation and recognition from others, they develop a sense of animosity.

Notwithstanding, numerous individuals characterized by an inflated sense of self and grandiosity do possess the capability to thrive as leaders within organizations and amass substantial wealth owing to their persuasive charm, audacity, and capacity for foresight. An example of this can be observed in various research findings which indicate that chief executive officers who exhibit narcissistic traits demonstrate a higher propensity for embracing significant strategic decisions. This encompasses ventures such as investing in innovative technology, venturing into global markets, and engaging in company acquisitions. However, it is important to note that studies have also demonstrated that individuals with grandiose narcissistic tendencies may jeopardize the advancement of their enterprises in favor of their personal agendas, presenting an unfavorable circumstance.

Due to the propensity of grandiose narcissists to exhibit impulsivity, excessive confidence, and a reluctance to take guidance from experts, they tend to consistently make poor decisions. They are disinclined to employ objectivity in reaching a conclusion due to an excessive sense of self-importance. They hold the belief that whatever choice they make must inherently possess goodness, regardless of any circumstances. Individuals with narcissistic tendencies may exhibit a heightened level of intuition compared to those without such tendencies, and this characteristic should not necessarily be deemed inappropriate or erroneous. Nevertheless, even a hint of understanding should be grounded in rationality and sound argumentation. Additionally, their inclination towards doubting others with regards to their knowledge, skills, and understanding reflects their lack of regard for the opinions of others. Their inflated sense of superiority and unwavering self-assurance hinder their inclination to engage with individuals from diverse backgrounds, comprehend alternate viewpoints, and embrace unorthodox concepts. They are capable of disregarding empirical evidence and research in order to assert their own desires and appease their personal egos.

Evasion of Responsibility and Lack of Willingness to Acquire Knowledge

Moreover, individuals tend to hold others accountable for unfavorable results without acknowledging their own role and exhibit a lack of interest in extracting valuable lessons from their past shortcomings. However, if they achieve success, they have a tendency to solely claim credit and fail to adequately acknowledge the contributions of others. On every occasion of their victory, they desire to utilize it as a platform to exhibit their sense of superiority. Nonetheless, they perceive experiencing loss as indicative of vulnerability, hence they exhibit a reluctance to scrutinize the underlying factors contributing to failure and display a lack of propensity for gaining knowledge from such situations. It proves challenging for them to reassess and enhance their cognitive discernment abilities.

Individuals with a tendency towards grandiose narcissism can also engage in the deliberate manipulation of others in order to further their personal interests.

In certain circumstances, individuals may resort to falsehoods, deception, and unlawful acts in order to gratify their personal fantasies. They perceive themselves as supremely superior and exclusive, resulting in their engagement in various self-centered and inconsiderate behaviors.

How Can You Leave That Toxic Relationship Even When You're Still In Love With Your Partner?

In certain situations, advantageous elements have a tendency to undergo self-destruction so as to pave the way for the emergence of more favorable circumstances.

Why does it cause such intense pain?

You appear to be deeply captivated, however, your relationship has developed into an unhealthy state. It can't proceed.

Following a considerable lapse of time subsequent to an agitated evening, you find yourself reclining while mentally revisiting the conflicts.

One may find it challenging to grasp the underlying rationale behind their partner's unwillingness to alter their behavior or their apparent disregard for one's emotional well-being. Please reflect upon whether they truly harbored genuine affection for you at any moment.

You have made numerous attempts to salvage your relationship, but thus far, none have proven successful. You are aware that the present moment presents an opportune occasion to conclude this, however, the prospect of being distanced from all others immobilizes you.

However, the level of aggravation has reached an unbearable extent. If you fail to cease this endeavor promptly, you may risk significant personal detriment.

1. Exploring Strategies for Release

Letting go of someone you have affection for is undoubtedly a formidable undertaking.

I had to acknowledge that my relationship with my ex wasn't intended to be.

The complete deceit and dishonesty proved to be overwhelmingly burdensome for me to handle. Moreover, to aggravate the situation, he was indeed oppressive towards me as well.

The strikes were extraordinarily unexpected. I could not ascertain with certainty whether the ensuing contention would result in my admission to the medical facility, or, perhaps more direly, prove fatal for me.

I held the conviction that he would refrain from causing harm to me. I have faith that he has the capacity to understand that his actions deeply shattered me.

I held the belief that he possessed the capacity for change.

Regardless of whether I possessed the title of the foremost lady or the dearest companion on earth, no measure of effort would have produced any outcome.

Can it be confirmed that he was genuinely deserving of all the recognition bestowed upon him?

No, he wasn't. Furthermore, it dawned upon me that I had harbored an anticipation of removing him from my existence.

If you happen to find yourself ensnared in a detrimental relationship, it is imperative that you acknowledge your capacity to regain your self-worth and move forward independently.

2. Understand That You Merit Better

Occasionally, merely having affection for someone is insufficient if it is not reciprocated in the same manner.

It is analogous to expending diligence on an antiquated, immobilized automobile. No matter the amount of physical exertion and emotional investment you dedicate to the task at hand, it cannot be reversed or undone starting from this point forward.

The time you waste on an unsuitable individual hinders the arrival of the ideal person into your life.

In what manner could they enter your life, considering that the aforementioned vacancy is already occupied?

It necessitated a substantial commitment of time and effort on my part in order to truly grasp this concept.

Had you informed me at that time, that I could encounter an individual who would sincerely love and profoundly respect me for my authentic self, I would never have placed any confidence in your words.

I found it necessary to relinquish.

Shortly after severing ties with my unhealthy relationship, I encountered my significant other. He is the reason I wholeheartedly believe in authentic love in the present day.

I serve as irrefutable proof that one can indeed experience authentic love if they merely embrace the belief that a superior counterpart awaits them.

One might be unaware of their true identity or the timing of their arrival, nevertheless, they vigilantly await the moment when you surrender so they can enter your existence.

3. Do not rely on the belief that your partner will undergo a transformation.

Opting to continue a relationship where one is subjected to abuse constitutes the gravest error that an individual can commit.

It is imperative for you to recognize that the primary entity under your control within this world is your own self.

Unless the other individual acknowledges responsibility for their mistakes and demonstrates a willingness to seek assistance, it is unlikely that they will undergo any transformation.

They may commit to transitioning and intensifying efforts to enhance the situation.

They may endeavor to be precise in conveying their expectations at that juncture.

However, undoubtedly, circumstances will remain somewhat alike, especially if they have previously made commitments which they failed to fulfill.

Transformation must originate from within; Only then can circumstances truly be resolved.

I held the belief that my former partner would undergo a transformation on account of my influence. That was my conviction, under the assumption that I exerted sufficient effort in conveying the extent of the pain he caused me, thereby leaving him with no viable alternative but to initiate a change. Yet, I was off-base.

Occasionally, our discernment becomes clouded. Occasionally, it is imperative for us to perceive the utmost potential in an individual. Occasionally, we experience a profound fear of being apart from our beloved.

Despite all that we tell ourselves, certain relationships are irreparable.

4. Recognize That It Will Cause Pain

There is no straightforward method for circumventing it.

It will hurt. Additionally, there is a significant amount of harm occurring.

You are experiencing anxiety due to the absence of the feeling of being valued and necessary, the intimate and affectionate moments that were once shared.

Instead of being merely a fragment of your existence, they have become an integral part of your entire life. You have neglected to recall the importance of prioritizing your own well-being.

The most challenging aspect lies in transcending the intrinsic anguish associated with the state of isolation from one's counterparts. Nevertheless, once one progresses beyond that phase, existence becomes markedly more uncomplicated.

The illustrations you present along the way will enable you to cultivate and enhance your personal growth.

The annoyance will not persevere indefinitely. Time serves as the most cherished of companions.

When I terminated my friendship with my former partner, I diligently attempted various strategies to keep myself preoccupied. Based on a logical assessment, it is my conclusion that the vexation would ultimately dissipate.

When that approach proved unsuccessful, I endeavored to strategize methods aimed at repairing our relationship rather than terminating it. I determined that accepting his failure was more manageable than experiencing profound loneliness.

That was yet another futile attempt to distance oneself from sorrow.

In due time, I came to the realization that I had to acknowledge the inherent impossibility of its success, and that any strategy I pursued to terminate it would undoubtedly entail complexity.

By adopting the approach of confronting rather than avoiding physiological distress, you mitigate the potential consequences of unaddressed emotions afflicting you in the future.

5. Incorporate the Act of Weeping as a Solution

The most prudent course of action for your own benefit would be to address the frustration. Refrain from suppressing or containing it.

On certain occasions, it is expected of us to leverage our strengths while addressing challenging situations.

I perceive that as lacking capability.

The more I exerted effort in containing my tears and maintaining composure, the more negative I experienced, ultimately causing deep distress.

What was my response?

I cried.

I cried again

And again

Subsequently, I shed additional tears.

Indeed, you have understood me correctly.

I sobbed hysterically!

I ceased envisioning a state of complete contentment. I consciously permitted the tears to persist until reaching the point where I perceived them incapable of shedding further. It endured half a month, however I embraced a new lease on life when it was finished.

The customary sensation of constriction in my chest had dissipated. I began to engage in more discerning thought and discerned that circumstances were not inherently as dire as my initial assumptions had led me to believe.

I resumed wearing a smile upon my face. I initiated the observation of the sun's sparkling radiance and the enchanting vapors in the sky. I was not currently situated in that monotonous location. I genuinely experienced a complete sense of rejuvenation.

Instead of trying to focus on my strengths, I can offer assistance in the improvement of the system.

6. Go on vacation

Occasionally, there are moments that give the impression of an impending catastrophe, albeit it is not the case.

Your mind's inclination to engage in prank-like behaviors has become increasingly absurd, making it implausible to continue believing in its ability to deliver happiness.

However, that isn't correct.

Often, the most effective solution to anguish is the passage of time.

Through providing a period of respite for your heart, mind, and spirit, you afford yourself the chance to rejuvenate. This also presents an ideal occasion for acquainting myself with you.

Perchance there exists a secondary passion that brings you joy or an activity you hold in high regard.

In my personal perspective, sewing was the case. Notwithstanding the aforementioned limitation of not completely disengaging my mind, it granted me the opportunity to spend time in solitude while engaging in an activity that brought me genuine enjoyment.

In addition, that is what I esteemed.

Ultimately, my focus shifted more towards self-reflection, directing less attention towards my external circumstances.

Despite not producing immediate results, it proved immensely beneficial over an extended period of time.

If you grant permission, each day will gradually become more manageable. Time mends.

Despite the unexpected failure of my relationship, I realized that I could still actively engage in my life.

Self-Esteem Vs. Narcissism

In consideration of the current emphasis on nurturing self-care, it is imperative to elucidate the discernment between possessing robust self-assurance and exuding narcissistic inclinations. Ultimately, it is customary within society, specifically in metropolitan areas, to possess a significant level of self-assurance. It facilitates success in job interviews, fosters professional connections, and enables efficient completion of numerous daily responsibilities, rendering it wholly acceptable. It constitutes an inherent facet of our individual characters, an instinctual response essential for our survival. Nonetheless, when an individual begins to engage in manipulative behavior or any other form of negativity solely for their own gratification, they are venturing into the malevolent realm of narcissism.

In more explicit terms, the essence of possessing a healthy self-esteem entails the capability to uphold self-respect. In contrast, narcissism revolves around the pursuit of acknowledgement stemming from an innate desire for attention and admiration. For individuals with narcissistic tendencies, these substances act as potent stimulants, and in the event of dwindling resources, they will promptly employ diverse methods to secure further supplies.

An individual with robust self-esteem derives their confidence intrinsically, whereas the narcissist relies on external validation for their sense of well-being. Possessing self-worth is rooted in recognizing one's values and honoring exemplary figures, whereas narcissism compels individuals to establish unattainable expectations for themselves and those in their vicinity. Narcissistic individuals have a tendency to hold high regard for public figures who exhibit comparable personality attributes. Narcissism revolves around envy, where competition and comparison serve as the underlying principles. A narcissistic individual typically gravitates towards a dictator-like role, whereas an individual with sound self-esteem tends to value cooperation and equality.

Possessing self-esteem entails maintaining confidence in oneself without resorting to boasting about one's capabilities, whereas narcissism involves engaging in ostentatious behavior and belittling others in order to enhance one's perceived importance in the eyes of others.

Development of Narcissism vs. Self-Esteem

Offspring whose parents bestowed praise upon them regardless of their level of exertion are predisposed to develop narcissistic tendencies. Children of this kind were brought up with a constant need to seek validation and accolades from others, making it their utmost priority.

Nonetheless, offspring who were nurtured by parents who sincerely acknowledged their behaviors would acquire a profound understanding of their own identity and environment, ultimately fostering a positive level of self-assurance.

Based on research findings, it is crucial to refrain from bestowing unfounded praises upon children for aptitudes they lack or for proficiencies they have yet to develop, as a preventive measure against fostering narcissistic tendencies. It is imperative to duly acknowledge their genuine accomplishments so as to enhance their sense of self-worth.

Naturally, it is not only the parents who can be held accountable for the cultivation of narcissistic traits. The culture of each society also plays a crucial role. A society encompasses distinct cultural and social norms that can evoke varying degrees of self-esteem within individuals. An individual might inadvertently establish excessively lofty standards for themselves, subsequently experiencing disillusionment and resorting to various coping mechanisms, including the development of narcissistic tendencies.

For example, in many regions of the Western world, a man is expected to possess considerable wealth and achieve notable success, whereas a woman is anticipated to possess youthfulness and physical attractiveness considered as an "ideal." These ideas can have severe effects on children, and coupled with other influences surrounding them, these ideals will affect how children view themselves and others.

Fostering a Positive Self-Image as an Alternative to Narcissism

The initial step you must undertake is to discern recurring patterns in your conduct. Give consideration to the most recent instance in which you inflicted harm upon another individual or contemplate your response to receiving criticism. Did you adopt a defensive stance and commence the act of rationalizing your actions? Individuals with narcissistic tendencies have a proclivity to suppress thoughts and behaviors that elicit feelings of insecurity. However, to cultivate a positive self-image, it is necessary to approach it from an unbiased standpoint and hold oneself accountable for any errors in order to extract valuable lessons from such encounters.

Acquire the ability to demonstrate heightened sensitivity and empathy towards the emotions and experiences of others. For instance, demonstrate greater patience towards individuals who may not grasp a concept as swiftly as you did, rather than reveling in your own superiority.

An individual is educated throughout their lifetime to engage in combat for the purpose of survival, and making constant efforts to enhance one's own abilities has become the prevailing standard. Although this is not entirely unfavorable, individuals should refrain from excessively criticizing themselves due to setbacks and perceived flaws. In such a manner, the cultivation of a positive self-regard is facilitated while the promotion of self-centeredness is deterred.

They lack compassion.

Walfish posits that a key characteristic of narcissists is their incapacity to comprehend the emotions experienced by others. Individuals with narcissistic personality disorder frequently encounter challenges when it comes to articulating remorse and comprehending the perspectives and opinions of others.

According to the author, narcissists demonstrate an inability to comprehend the concept of emotions, resulting in a deficiency in acknowledging, affirming, comprehending, or embracing your experiences.

Do the disagreements between your parents, conflicts with your best friend, or challenging professional experiences exert an influence on your relationship with your partner? If you articulate the factors that evoke anger and sadness, do they become disinterested?

According to Walfish, the ultimate deterioration of a relationship often stems from the deficiency of empathy or sympathy exhibited by individuals with NPD, regardless of whether the relationship is of a romantic nature or not.

They possess a limited number (if at all) of enduring friendships.

Individuals diagnosed with Narcissistic Personality Disorder (NPD) often face frequent conflicts and discord with those around them. Upon further examination of their relationships, it becomes evident that they possess a limited number of intimate acquaintances.

Furthermore, individuals afflicted with Narcissistic Personality Disorder may manifest characteristics of heightened sensitivity and insecurity. They may experience anger if your intention is to socialize with other individuals.

They possess the ability to level allegations against you for insufficiently allocating time to their presence, inducing feelings of guilt in your social interactions with acquaintances, or passing judgments on the nature of friendships you maintain.

They incessantly target and torment you.

Possibly, it originated as playful banter but swiftly transitioned into malicious behavior. Suddenly, they have developed a heightened sensitivity to your choices and actions, encompassing your attire, diet, companions, and television preferences.

Antagonism and enmity are widely recognized attributes.

Individuals diagnosed with Narcissistic Personality Disorder (NPD) exert a pronounced deleterious influence on those around them.

According to Peykar, they will subject you to insults, employ derogatory language, deliver sharp remarks, and make humorous jests. Their objective is to diminish the self-esteem of others in order to enhance their own, as this grants them a perception of authority.

In addition, addressing their statements may inadvertently validate their behavior. According to Peykar, a narcissist derives pleasure from receiving a reaction. According to Peykar, a narcissist seeks gratification through eliciting a response. This is because it serves as evidence of their capacity to evoke an emotional response in others.

Should you be subjected to an attack upon the achievement of a noteworthy milestone, promptly depart the vicinity.

A narcissistic individual may put forth an explanation, such as "Your success was attributable to my insufficient sleep," in an attempt to create an impression that you held an unfair advantage over them.

They desire for you to comprehend that you do not possess a higher status than them. Due to the fact that nobody is subordinate to them.

Chapter Two –

Causes

It is evident to you that narcissistic personality entails a profound absence of empathy towards others, along with a sustained inclination towards grandiosity and a constant desire for admiration from others. Individuals with this personality trait hold the conviction that they represent the utmost significance in the lives of every person they encounter. Whilst this conduct may be deemed suitable for individuals of noble lineage, it is not deemed acceptable in broader societal circles.

Individuals who possess this disorder will exhibit an air of contempt and haughtiness, thereby potentially projecting an attitude of condescension. One possible alternative in a formal tone could be: "They might express their dissatisfaction with the incompetence of a waiter or waitress in an impolite manner, or they might harbor the belief that they possess the capacity to make medical judgments without the expertise of a qualified physician."

What is the underlying cause of this phenomenon?

Etiology of Narcissistic Personality Disorder.

Regrettably, the precise etiology of narcissism remains largely elusive. Scientists are currently engaged in ongoing investigations to elucidate the precise etiology in order to develop effective therapeutic interventions for the ailment. There exist various theories regarding the potential origins of the disorder. These theories aim to provide insights into identifying its root causes and developing appropriate treatment approaches for it.

The initial hypothesis posits that narcissism is a physiological or hereditary ailment. Instances have been observed in which the guardians of children exhibiting narcissistic traits possess narcissistic tendencies themselves. As a result, certain researchers postulate that narcissism may be heritable, transmitted from one parent to their offspring, and subsequently perpetuated.

The second hypothesis posits that narcissism is an outcome of environmental influences stemming from problematic interactions between a child and their parents. Researchers posit that parent-child relationships characterized by either excessive indulgence or excessive censure could exacerbate or precipitate the problem. This social or environmental theory can also be posited in light of the observation that children exhibiting this inclination also demonstrate a parallel manifestation of such behaviors in their parents. Hence, one could contend that narcissism is a behavior acquired through the process of learning.

The third hypothesis posits that narcissism may be attributed to psychological factors originating from childhood personality and temperament conditions, misguided parental teachings, and acquired coping mechanisms in response to stress.

Undoubtedly, the fourth hypothesis posits that the interplay of these three factors contributes to the emergence of narcissistic tendencies. The prevailing belief among the scientific community and scholarly researchers is that the development of this ailment can be attributed to a combination of factors, namely genetics, societal norms, and environmental influences. Nevertheless, research indicates that in the event an individual is afflicted with this disorder or any other personality disorder, there is a likelihood of its hereditary transmission to their offspring. The ambiguity surrounding the transmission of this trait, be it through genetic factors or acquired behavior, remains undocumented.

Fortunately, it is worth noting that genuine narcissistic personality disorder is actually a rather uncommon occurrence. Adolescents may exhibit indications and characteristics associated with narcissism; however, it is imperative to recognize that such behavioral patterns are often a natural manifestation of their developmental stage and do not necessarily indicate a propensity towards developing narcissistic personality disorder in the future. Nevertheless, the disorder will commence during the late adolescence and early adulthood stages, exacerbating in proximity to the age of thirty and subsequently attenuating beyond the age of forty.

Although the exact cause remains uncertain, there is a school of thought suggesting that a biological element in children renders them particularly vulnerable to excessive or delayed admiration, potentially leading to the development of a personality disorder later in life. The child has the potential to cultivate a diminished sense of self-worth, which they may conceal through the cultivation of an artificial facade of flawlessness, coupled with behavior aimed at garnering continual recognition.

While the root cause remains undetermined, it is unequivocally established that the diagnosis of narcissism is firm and irrefutable. Continue reading to discover additional information!

Types Of Narcissists

The Narcissist Exhibiting Vulnerability and Invulnerability

Vulnerable. These individuals exhibiting narcissistic traits are those who have undergone distressing circumstances. They typically exhibit a high level of self-awareness and caution when it comes to placing their trust in others, which may be perceived as introversion. Nevertheless, they are profoundly influenced by their previous experiences, resulting in a simultaneous apprehension of being abandoned and rejected. Consequently, they are emotionally detached, unable to experience love, exhibit affection, or reciprocate in a similar manner. They possess a delicate disposition prone to taking offense, yet have fortified their emotions with barriers to safeguard themselves, thereby presenting a distorted image that they wish others to perceive. To an extent, the vulnerable narcissist wants to believe this too. They harbor internal sensations of insignificance - they perceive themselves as lacking ability and merit. This translates into their profound ability to pull the strings, manipulate, and lie. They frequently employ manipulative tactics to elicit feelings of guilt in others, actively pursue sympathy and exclusive attention, and are reluctant to publicly criticize or reproach you. Similarly, they are incapable of recognizing your worth.

Invulnerable. We are familiar with these individuals who display narcissistic traits, being of the narcissistic persuasion. They exhibit a pronounced sense of self-assurance, a penchant for arrogance, and an inclination towards aggression, rendering them highly immoral individuals that should be meticulously evaded. They perceive themselves as nothing less than a benevolent contribution to the human race. They, similar to individuals categorized as vulnerable narcissists, demonstrate a complete lack of consideration for your feelings, emotions, and circumstances. They exhibit condescending behavior, which frequently leads us to question their capacity for empathy and their excessive focus on themselves, to the detriment of our well-being and that of others. Invulnerable narcissists are individuals of authoritative nature who display a fervent desire to maintain unyielding control and dominion over all aspects of their surroundings. They experience a sense of superiority that leads them to believe they have the right to assume a position of leadership. They aspire to stand out conspicuously in a given space, lacking any form of moderation or restraint. Associated with the absence of a filter is an impression that they lack emotion; they exhibit a detached and unfeeling demeanor, apparently impervious to any criticism directed their way.

Elitist Narcissist

These are individuals who exhibit a sense of entitlement and hold the belief that they are inherently superior to others. These individuals with narcissistic tendencies have achieved numerous remarkable milestones throughout their lives, ascending to the highest positions solely by displacing others. These individuals do not exhibit the qualities of collaborative team members, whether in professional endeavors or personal relationships. They will enthusiastically extol and confidently showcase all of their accomplishments. They perceive themselves as distinctive as a result of the acknowledgment they have attained, and to some extent, they anticipate universal recognition for the awards, accomplishments, or any other endeavors they have successfully pursued.

Malignant Narcissist

This is unquestionably the most perilous category of narcissist, commonly found in connection with illicit behavior, gang-related pursuits, and involvement in the consumption or trafficking of controlled substances. They exhibit traits reminiscent of psychopathy and demonstrate a complete absence of ethical values. All that is considered favorable and unfavorable is ultimately beneficial. Their demeanor is devoid of basic human kindness, as they exhibit excessive arrogance, aggression, and a conspicuous absence of remorse for their misdeeds. Consequently, interacting with or associating oneself with such individuals becomes an extremely perilous and daunting endeavor. Where might we locate these individuals? Correctional facilities, rehabilitation centers, and similar establishments.

Amorous Narcissist

These individuals characterized by narcissistic traits possess a heightened degree of sexuality. A few individuals among us possess knowledge on the matter. They frequently engage in the act of boastfully discussing their sexual encounters, whether concerning themselves or their previous partners. They can be characterized as deviant and excessively focused on sexual matters. Amorous narcissists are also materialistic individuals and will often be blinded by money, or rather, as we call them, money-grabbers, and gold-diggers. Due to their aesthetically pleasing appearance, they possess the ability to effortlessly convince and allure you, with the ultimate intention of determining their true target. They are individuals who engage in casual encounters and have a tendency to promise follow-up communication. They possess a proclivity for public display of their bodies and engage in sensual behavior.

Opinionated Narcissist

That their perspective is the appropriate one and the sole perspective that warrants consideration. This can be rather exasperating, however, this is simply a reflection of their inherent nature. We undoubtedly are acquainted with individuals of pronounced opinions and narcissistic tendencies, whether encountered within the professional sphere or in the realm of our familial relationships. These opinions encompass a range of topics, spanning from recommendations on personal care products such as shampoo and cologne, to advice on financial management.

Humiliation Narcissist

This is the type of narcissist that can be encountered ubiquitously, spanning across educational institutions and professional environments. They epitomize the role of aggressors, individuals who derive satisfaction from degrading and undermining others. They engage in this behavior intuitively, as though it serves as a means to restore their sense of self-assurance and self-worth, all the while captivating their acquaintances - their ardent followers.

Compensatory Narcissist

These individuals with narcissistic tendencies exhibit a pessimistic perspective concerning their own character traits. They possess numerous vulnerabilities, which they deliberately conceal through the tactic of deflection. They are frustrated individuals. What is commonly referred to as passive-aggressive behavior.

Grandiose Narcissist

These individuals, as indicated by the aforementioned heading, exhibit a predisposition for unabashedly flaunting their accomplishments and triumphs. They seek to ensure that all individuals are aware of their exceptional qualities.

Narcissistic personality disorder has the potential to profoundly distort one's cognitive processes, leading to a highly singular and polarizing worldview. This occurrence is observed among a vast number of individuals globally. However, what makes this disorder of such paramount significance? Indeed, this phenomenon has a greater impact on individuals other than the narcissists themselves. It pertains to a condition in which one individual harbors a superiority complex while perceiving a deficiency in the other individual, causing a noticeable psychological impact on both parties involved. However, the concept of segregating narcissists from others is a distinct idea that merits further examination.

Relationships. This is an essential human requirement that hinges upon interpersonal connectivity. Furthermore, individuals with narcissistic tendencies, while recognizing the importance of healthy interpersonal bonds and the ensuing exchanges, encounter difficulties in maintaining substantial intimate relationships as a result of the inherent "true nature" that resides within them. The inherent essence of a narcissist has the potential to drain the vibrancy from another individual's existence. Narcissistic individuals often display a fundamental disinterest in our emotional well-being, as we are well aware. However, for individuals who have been in a romantic partnership with a narcissist, we have acquired knowledge of their cognitive patterns and mindset, primarily through direct personal encounters. We also empathize with the anguish, despondency, and frequently demoralizing sentiments of realizing that we have squandered time with that individual. They exploit our resources and siphon off our vitality.

Individuals with narcissistic traits often exhibit a diminished sense of self-worth, a characteristic that can be readily linked to their upbringing and personal experiences. The maltreatment that they endured during their formative years, encompassing both psychological and physical harm. They adopt a facade in order to conceal their imperfections, implying a heightened sense of self-consciousness that compels them to present a modified image of themselves on a daily basis. What are their deficiencies? Empathy.

Individuals involved in a romantic partnership with a narcissistic individual often experience a pervasive sentiment of degradation. In the initial stages of the relationship, the narcissist exhibited charm, wit, and a notable level of compassion. Hence, we fell for the trap and committed ourselves to their cause. But they changed. The courtship was remarkable; however, the subsequent bond gradually deteriorated as the individual with whom we were deeply infatuated became increasingly aloof. Maybe too comfortable. They deliberately disregarded our presence, subjected us to embarrassment, and promptly highlighted each and every one of our mistakes - a comprehensive account that appeared to encompass every single aspect. It proved to be an exceedingly arduous task to be in their company, yet due to their manipulation tactics and incessant dishonesty, we naively believed we could rectify their behavior. Get them back. This is the factor that caused us fatigue and initiated a transformation within us. We experienced immense self-doubt, leading us to perceive ourselves as inadequate. The problems that they faced ultimately became our collective concerns, evolving into significantly greater sources of distress that we are currently compelled to endure. However, we are fine; we have persevered. It has come to our understanding that we are no longer the individuals responsible for the aforementioned circumstances. it's them.

Presented below are a set of inquiries designed to evaluate one's degree of narcissism within the context of an intimate and romantic partnership. These principles are pertinent to both the individual exhibiting narcissistic traits and the individual experiencing distress within that interpersonal dynamic. Each of these inquiries pertains to a binary response. There are additional online resources available that can provide you with an answer regarding your level of narcissism. Have fun!

1) In the pursuit of a romantic partnership, would you prioritize being with an aesthetically pleasing individual

with whom you lack chemistry, or with someone less physically attractive who will offer you genuine affection and devotion?

2) Do you have a preference for financially prosperous individuals of the opposite/same gender?

3) Are you inclined towards assuming the dominant role within the context of the relationship?

4) Are you interested in pursuing a transitory association that solely caters to your own interests, or are you inclined towards establishing a lasting partnership characterized by both positive and challenging experiences?

5) Are you willing to listen to your partner when he/she has a concern and then to make the effort to make sure that your partner does not have to feel that concern again?

6) Are you of the opinion that a relationship possesses enduring qualities?

7) Are you inclined to exert influence over your partner in order to derive personal advantage?

8) Are you inclined to display affection towards your significant other?

9) Have you ever experienced a moment in any previous or ongoing relationship where you derived pleasure from instilling a sense of guilt in your partner?

10) Have you ever coerced your significant other into performing a task by creating the impression that it was essential?

11) Have you ever employed ultimatums by threatening to terminate the relationship if your partner did not fulfill a specific request or brought up an issue?

12) Are you prone to shifting the responsibility for your own mistakes onto your partner?

13) In your judgment, do you believe that you bring happiness to your partner?

14) If not, do you anticipate the possibility of this occurring in the future?

15) Is your partner disregarding your emotions?

16) Does your partner exhibit behavior towards individuals of the opposite gender that elicits feelings of jealousy within you?

17) Have you ever cheated on your partner and blamed them for the reason as to why you have cheated?

18) Are you of the opinion that your significant other is engaging in infidelity?

Could you kindly share the aspect of your relationship with your partner that you find most enjoyable?

Are you open to accepting the possibility of being incorrect if it leads to your partner's perspective being valid?

Dealing With Vanity

If you possess the ability to comprehend the concept of splitting, you are making significant progress towards enhancing your capability to effectively address the majority of challenging human conduct. Characteristics within the realm of vanity encompass the inclination of the narcissist to exert influence upon others, compelling them to partake in the process of segregating the world into esteemed (flawless or "admirable") and disparaged (insignificant or "inferior") classifications. These designations serve as manifestations of the internal schisms inherent to the narcissistic individual. Anything that does not meet the highest standards holds no value. Narcissists crave reassurance of being perceived as faultless. They seek to evoke admiration or instill envy within you. This persistent strain occupies a considerable amount of emotional capacity within any interpersonal connection. Additionally, it can induce a sense of destabilization in one's perception of oneself and the surrounding world. Similar to how extended exposure to an individual who incessantly voices grievances can elicit feelings of frustration, negativity, and helplessness, engaging in a partnership with a person who extensively employs splitting can gradually lead to perceiving oneself and others through a dichotomous lens of positivity and negativity.

Exercise caution regarding the poles.

Polarized cognition and emotions can yield unforeseen consequences. One may experience a decrease in self-assurance, heightened feelings of suspicion, and an increased sense of fear beyond their typical state. On occasion, there may arise a sense of powerlessness, insignificance, vulnerability, or susceptibility to domination. On alternative occasions, you may experience a state of considerable strength, excessive sense of responsibility, feelings of guilt, or a sense of exasperation. When there is a separation of one individual within a relationship, it frequently leads to a corresponding separation in the other party. As an illustration, in the event that a narcissistic individual harbors a sense of complete perfection, it can give rise to feelings of worthlessness and vulnerability in their partner. Therapists specialized in narcissism often encounter feelings of inadequacy, ineffectiveness, or incompetence when attempting to address the needs of grandiose narcissistic individuals. On the contrary, when interacting with individuals who exhibit vulnerable narcissistic tendencies, it is often typical to experience feelings of superiority, potency, and astuteness.

The fundamental approach to addressing splitting involves refraining from succumbing to the binary mindset of either/or. Remaining conscious of your emotional responses towards the narcissist proves to be an effective tactic. Reflect upon your emotional state at this moment by questioning, "What is my current disposition?" Am I experiencing a sense of heightened importance, authority, irritation, or remorse? Alternatively, am I experiencing sensations of insignificance, vulnerability, error, or guilt?" Being mindful of whether one is being idealized or devalued can assist in comprehending the modus operandi of the narcissist. It is also capable of aiding in the preservation of a comprehensive understanding of oneself and the other individual.

Partner or Ex-Partner

Individuals have a tendency to romanticize elements when embarking upon a relationship. The duration of the initial phase, commonly referred to as the "honeymoon period," can span from several weeks to multiple years. Throughout this period, individuals are inclined to perceive the relationship as flawless. The notion of an idealized love originating from a flawless companion is nearly indiscernible from the manner in which individuals with narcissistic tendencies construct fantasies revolving around absolute perfection. Numerous individuals seek out a new partner as a source of narcissistic gratification, wherein they actively seek adulation, compliments, and validation regarding their physical attractiveness and desirability. During this period, it is not uncommon for individuals to also encounter intense emotions of envy, perceiving others as aspiring to appropriate their recently attained state of bliss.

Regarding maladaptive narcissism, numerous manifestations of self-admiration may become apparent within the context of romantic or past romantic partnerships. Certain individuals with narcissistic tendencies may exert undue influence on their partners by seeking perpetual confirmation of their worth. Some individuals employ their partners as a means of demonstrating their social standing or prestige. In certain interpersonal dynamics, issues may arise regarding sexual and emotional intimacy when the narcissistic partner does not perceive a sufficient level of admiration and appreciation.

Furthermore, envy has the potential to evolve into an extremely detrimental element.

If you perceive that the tendencies to idealize and devalue are having adverse implications on your relationship, it might be necessary for you to directly address these behaviors and question your partner's perceptions. Once more, it is advisable to exercise patience and choose a neutral moment when the situation is tranquil in order to accomplish this task effectively. It is imperative that you assume responsibility for your emotions by articulating them in a manner that reflects personal sentiments.

Primarily, strive to refrain from categorizing individuals into positive and negative aspects, including oneself. Regularly assess your emotional state by conducting self-evaluations. If an observable division or contrast is apparent, endeavor to shift towards a moderate or neutral position. In the event that you come to recognize your partner as exhibiting bullying behavior, make an effort to recall the admirable traits that initially attracted you to them. In the event that you become aware of your own sense of insignificance and susceptibility, endeavor to recall that you possess a complete sense of self, bestowed with the capacity for resilience and fortitude.

Parent

Individuals desire parental admiration and idealization, thus making it particularly challenging when parents become the ones yearning for admiration. A prevailing concept within narcissism theories revolves around parents who employ their children to satisfy their own narcissistic desires. Regardless of intentionality, the reversal of the inherent parent-child dynamic has profoundly detrimental and enduring consequences. If you are perusing this literary work with a parent as your intended audience, it is likely that circumstances have persisted in this manner for a considerable duration. It is hard to confront the status quo, especially when you are trying to change relationship patterns that have been in place for years.

When considering the implementation of alterations within a relationship, it is occasionally necessary for the majority of efforts to occur internally, within oneself. Consider the manner in which you actively engage in supporting your parent's pursuit of narcissistic validation. Do you tend to offer insincere compliments in response to pressure? Do you frequently experience a sense of duty to allow your parent to take center stage? Do you often endure discomfort while listening to self-indulgent speeches that trigger memories of being undervalued, excluded, and neglected during your childhood? In the event that this is the case, you are essentially actively engaging in perpetuating a relationship pattern that is detrimental to your well-being.

Elucidating the Vulnerable Nature of Self-Esteem

Many writers were captivated by the seeming paradox of delicate high self-confidence. In what manner can an individual exhibit excessive confidence while concurrently harboring feelings of insecurity and vulnerability?

The initial model we shall elucidate traces its origins back to psychoanalysis, commonly known as the mask model. Within the context of the non-psychoanalytical school of thought, this particular construct is commonly referred to as the incongruity between explicit and implicit self-esteem; however, it is imperative to note that these two designations essentially connote identical concepts.

Based on the mask model, the outward depiction of confidence, self-worth, and grandiosity in certain individuals serves as a mere semblance, concealing a less desirable inner reality for the person in question. The outer facade of stability is a distinct form of reactive formation, as it shields underlying feelings of insecurity and a lack of self-assurance with outward displays of grandeur and strength.

The origin of the mask model has been credited to two prominent clinicians, Heinz Kohut and Otto Kernberg.

It can be reasonably inferred that this mask model holds substantial relevance in elucidating the vulnerable subtype of narcissism. However, it appears to be ineffective in the context of the grandiose subtype. Consequently, numerous studies conducted in an attempt to investigate the purported association between implicit insecurity and narcissism have yielded inconclusive results - at times, it appeared that narcissism is indeed connected to implicit insecurity, whereas other studies were unable to replicate these findings. In succinct terms, it can be deduced that the mask model fails to encompass the entirety of potential narcissistic expressions.

The following theory, known as the unstable self-esteem theory, was introduced by Kernis, Grannemann, and Barclay in the year 1989. The authors refrained from employing the differentiation between the implicit and explicit selves, upon which the mask model is founded. Per Kernis and his colleagues, individuals with unstable self-esteem exhibit heightened receptivity to evaluative feedback, a propensity to attribute both positive and negative experiences to themselves, and increased preoccupation with self-perception.

The aforementioned perspective on the matter is of notable interest due to its empirical nature, wherein the theory is substantiated by scientific data. As an illustration, Kernis postulated that the fluctuation of the ego is the factor which influences the levels of anger and hostility, rather than the magnitude of self-esteem (whether high or low). Alternatively, one might state: "To phrase it more precisely, the interplay between the degree and durability of self-esteem impacts the manifestation of anger and hostility within a specific context."

It is postulated that individuals exhibiting high levels of fluctuating self-esteem are more susceptible to engage in violent and hostile behaviors when compared to those possessing consistently high levels of self-esteem. The rationale underpinning this determination is as follows: according to Kernis, Grannemann, and Barclay (1989), there exists a direct correlation between the extent of damage and the urgency of restoration. 1014). It goes without saying that individuals possessing a fragile sense of self-worth, such as those with narcissistic tendencies, are significantly more prone to perceiving certain circumstances as detrimental. These individuals have much at stake should they permit reality to triumph over their grandiose notions. Restoration encompasses all endeavors aimed at safeguarding the vulnerable and idealized portrayal of oneself. Occasionally, these endeavors culminate in highly aggressive actions.

Kernis' predictions were corroborated by numerous studies, indicating that individuals possessing elevated yet volatile self-esteem are considerably more prone to experiencing emotional responses such as anger and hostility in the presence of adversarial circumstances.

What is the underlying significance of all this? Do individuals characterized by high and enduring self-regard, who exhibit narcissistic tendencies, consistently portray themselves as affable and empathetic, actively engaging in altruistic endeavors across various global contexts? Unfortunately not. In Kernis' empirical investigations, the assessments of anger and hostility typically encompassed components of impulsive behavior. Stated differently, the predominant reaction to threats was carefully evaluated, whereas other equally or potentially more harmful occurrences such as resentment, contempt, and hate were regarded as secondary provisions.

Hence, it can be deduced that the assertion linking individuals possessing high and volatile levels of self-esteem to a tendency towards expressing anger should be limited to instances of impulsive and immediate reactions.

Narcissists with elevated and unwavering levels of self-esteem appear considerably more composed and composed, particularly in their external demeanor. When confronted with a challenge to their heightened self-perception, individuals often manifest emotions such as disdain and animosity. These feelings, although not inherently associated with immediate aggression, possess a much more covert and pernicious quality compared to the impulsive reactions often observed in individuals with vulnerable narcissism. When an individual harbors strong aversion towards someone, the process of preparing for revenge becomes significantly more methodical, deliberated upon, and strategically organized. Allow us to present an illustrative instance, the familiar acquaintance from our past, Charles Manson. Due to various circumstances, he harbored significant animosity towards the entire world. His extravagant notions were of such magnitude that he went so far as to devise a sect centered on the adoration of his extraordinary character. This individual may be appropriately characterized as a grandiose narcissist. All the assassinations he orchestrated were diligently strategized- every detail was thoroughly accounted for. A vulnerable narcissist is unlikely to exhibit such behavior; instead, they are more prone to engaging in outbursts of rage and subsequently settling down once the harm has been inflicted.

We opine that the differentiation between the two fundamental forms of narcissism has been somewhat elucidated at present. Additionally, it is important to reiterate that, although both categories possess a propensity for inflicting distress upon their surroundings, they diverge in their respective methods of expressing their hostility. In conclusion, this chapter aims to assert the significance of not succumbing to inflated assertions regarding narcissism propagated online. There exist individuals displaying narcissistic tendencies who experience distress and demonstrate a typical empathic reaction in select circumstances. Not every narcissist exhibits the traits of being cruel, abusive, or carrying out acts of violence and torture.

Narcissistic Fathers

This particular collective comprises individuals who exhibit a notable degree of self-centeredness, therefore warranting additional investigation. Taking the child's perspective into consideration holds particular significance. Subsequently, we shall witness the ramifications of a child's interpretation of their self-absorbed parents. Currently, we will adhere to delineating certain attributes of fathers with narcissistic tendencies, as well as their methods of projecting themselves onto their children.

To begin with, it should be noted that narcissistic fathers possess a substantial amount of charisma, or in the eyes of their children at least, they exude a compelling aura of charm and magnetism. Coupled with their self-assured and conceited demeanor, it is commonplace for children to deeply admire and idolize their parents, particularly fathers who frequently strive to be recognized as the family's patriarch.

Conversely, despite the profound admiration their children hold for them, narcissistic fathers engender fear while simultaneously exhibiting neglectful behavior and failing to be as present as they ought to be. This is the category of individuals who may undergo peculiar changes in their early forties, subsequently adopting a demeanor reminiscent of their teenage years. And this marks the specific period during which they demonstrate the utmost disregard for their children. It is evident that oftentimes individuals prioritize their own welfare over the welfare of their own offspring.

When faced with a challenge, paternal figures with narcissistic traits often exhibit a proclivity for engaging in an assertive outburst of anger that, despite being exclusively verbal, can inflict enduring emotional wounds upon their vulnerable offspring. We have consistently expressed that narcissists' most vulnerable area lies in their ability to handle criticism. Consider envisioning how narcissists respond when faced with opposition from their own offspring. Ultimately, they exercise absolute dominion over their children.

In addition to their frequent and extended absences, narcissistic fathers often exhibit a demeanor of detachment and remoteness, even when physically present. It appears as though they are leading distinct lives, independent of any connection to their children's lives. Indeed, they may offer occasional and notably lavish presents, however, establishing a profound connection on an emotional level proves to be an insurmountable challenge within the confines of this relationship.

While there are numerous methods by which a narcissistic father can inflict emotional harm upon his children, it is frequently asserted that distinctions exist in the dynamics of father-daughter and father-son relationships.

Connection with offspring - the progeny of a self-centered individual often perceives their association as partaking in an inequitable competition. There exists a divine being who consistently seizes every opportunity to boast about their magnificence and all-encompassing power. Young males who encounter such circumstances demonstrate a proclivity for cultivating a delicate and profoundly uncertain sense of self, as their fathers habitually subject them to intense criticism in an attempt to compensate for their own deficiencies through idolizing their offspring. This type of dynamic is observable in various settings, including playgrounds, where a father engages in recreational activities with his son, or at least appears to do so initially. Upon brief examination, it becomes evident that neither party is truly enjoying themselves. On one hand, there exists a father who endeavors to encourage his exceptionally talented son to engage in activities involving kicking or throwing a ball, while on the other hand, we observe a young child who grapples with striving to meet his father's aspirations. Genuine expressions of joy and lightheartedness are noticeably absent, all attention is focused on meticulously structured activities, each intended to pave the way for the child's eventual triumph. This particular scene serves as the quintessence of the deep-rooted dysfunctionality within the complicated dynamic between fathers exhibiting narcissistic traits and their sons.

The dynamics of attachment between daughters and narcissistic fathers exhibit some divergence, as daughters may perceive a noticeable absence of their father's presence, which falls short of their expectations. While this may occasionally be true in a literal sense, it is possible for the father to be present and yet, ultimately, a sense of unease persists. An illustration of this can be seen in the case of a narcissistic individual, who may excessively idealize their son to the point of neglecting their daughter.

We endeavor to illustrate at least one manifestation of a paternal narcissistic tendency by referencing the story of John Lennon. More precisely, it pertains to the manner in which he established a bond with his eldest offspring. Initially, it is imperative to acknowledge that during this particular timeframe, John Lennon was still relatively youthful, being around the ages of 26 to 27, while concurrently, the Beatles themselves were experiencing the pinnacle of their renown, specifically in the years 1966 and 1967. Regrettably, it was during this period that John Lennon engaged in extensive experimentation with drugs, particularly LSD. Coupled with his extravagant self-regard, as it undeniably was, alongside the renowned remark made by John Lennon in 1966—"We now surpass Jesus"—and the extravagant gatherings being held, the foremost member of the Beatles found himself lacking sufficient time to devote to his son, Julian Lennon. John Lennon exhibited severe mistreatment towards his former spouse, Cynthia Powell, who is also the mother of their son, Sean. Ultimately, in 1968 their marriage was formally dissolved, following which the renowned Beatle displayed an even greater disregard for Julian. This fact was truly evident to the extent that it caught the attention of Paul McCartney, a fellow member of The Beatles, who expressed sympathy towards the young Julian Lennon. The song "Hey Jude" by McCartney, which stands as one of the most celebrated achievements of The Beatles, was notably dedicated to Julian. When examined through this lens, the lyrics of the song appear to resemble a heartfelt entreaty aimed at the young man whom John Lennon disregarded throughout his lifetime. It appears as though Paul McCartney is expressing the following sentiment: "Although we are aware of the challenges associated with your current circumstances, it is essential to make an effort to overcome them." There will be improvement in the future."

Narcissistic Mother

In this discourse, our primary emphasis shall center around the dynamic that exists between a mother possessing narcissistic tendencies and her daughter. At the conclusion of the chapter, we will contemplate the potential patterns of bonding they cultivate with their sons.

In a previous section of the text, we have provided some information regarding narcissistic women and the dynamics within their family, specifically under the subheading "Female narcissist." Furthermore, it has been established that women exhibit a greater frequency of pro-social characteristics, including cooperation, warmth, emotional openness, and other dimensions outlined in the Big Five Model. It is not unexpected that daughters frequently develop considerably warmer and more intimate relationships with their mothers compared to their brothers. It is indeed more conceivable to envision a deep and close bond between a mother and daughter, as opposed to a son and his father, exhibiting a comparable level of intimacy. The male gender, on average, exhibits less emotional expression (although primarily on a superficial level) than the female gender. This discrepancy is highlighted as it signifies that daughters who have narcissistic mothers may be entangled in a relationship that is emotionally demanding and fraught with turbulence. From one perspective, self-centered mothers may exhibit an exceptional level of dedication towards the welfare of their daughters. To such an extent that their own self-importance becomes deeply entwined with every aspect of their daughter's life. From a psychoanalytical perspective, it can be observed that females with egocentric tendencies tend to project their own idealized self-image onto their daughters, perceiving them as ethereal beings embodying flawless qualities. An individual who is steadfastly loyal and assuredly dependable, consistently remaining by your side without any possibility of betrayal.

This glorification of the daughter has the ability to uphold the fabrication emanating from actuality, albeit temporarily. However, as adolescence commences, the idealized depictions of daughters disintegrate. Once her daughter displays signs of rebellion and detachment, which are common during the early stages of adolescence, the narcissistic mother promptly responds with excessive and stricter interventions.

To avoid being monotonous, we will employ the use of a concrete illustration. This is the account of an individual with whom we are acquainted - in fact, we have known this person since her early childhood. We witnessed the gradual unraveling of her life within a span of a few years. Based on Anna's own testimonies, it became evident that the relationship she had with her mother is far from being a wholesome one Her mother, whom we shall refer to as Tara.

Before delving into the crux of the narrative, it is imperative to provide a small caveat - John, Anna's father, was noticeably non-existent for the majority of her existence. Seldom did she have the chance to truly comprehend her father, and in general, their encounters were infrequent. Currently, Anna asserts that she lacks any concern regarding the opportunity to encounter John. We made no progress in eliciting from her even a speculative assessment of John's potential attributes, or any similar conjecture. To her, he epitomized the epitome of moral turpitude, a perambulator through existence devoid of even a modicum of awareness. As per Anna's account, he exploited her mother in the same manner as he does with any other women he encounters.

Contrastingly, Tara, her mother, was held in such high esteem and was often lauded to the extent that we envisioned a revered and refined entrepreneur, gracefully navigating from one important appointment to another. Tara epitomized qualities of autonomy, determination, and intellect. An individual to whom we can seek solace during challenging circumstances.

Regrettably, this was not entirely accurate. Tara could occasionally display profound compassion and endearment, yet it is conceivable that instances of indifference and covert disdain occurred as well. It is likely that Tara, preoccupied with her own issues and self-centered attachments, engaged in harmful behavior that inflicted considerable anguish upon Anna.

For instance, despite outwardly demonstrating a profound concern for her daughter's welfare, Tara consistently managed to disappoint her daughter during Anna's early years in high school. During the nascent stage of her life, Anna displayed certain portentous indications of personality disorders, albeit no definitive diagnosis was rendered at this juncture. However, her mother failed to exhibit a combination of warmth and authority in her response. Anna succumbed to substance abuse and was gradually spiraling into the abyss of this distressing and repulsive realm. However, Tara was not present. She was fervently constructing her own life anew, and above all, preoccupied with perpetually harboring frustration towards her defiant daughter. Undoubtedly, it is not uncommon for parents to experience anger occasionally. However, narcissistic mothers are inclined to harbor resentment towards their own children due to an excessive identification of their own egos with that of their children. The child's specific transgression is perceived as a direct affront. Something of considerable significance that is indelibly imprinted on one's memory. It is conceivable that Anna may have endured the effects of narcissistic abuse, as tacit animosity and neglect can also be classified as a type of maltreatment. Undoubtedly, intermittent instances of reciprocal verbal mistreatment were evident, serving only to perpetuate the situation. Due to the fact that the daughter's verbal insults act as the catalyst for her mother's narcissistic fury.

In the midst of such a familial ambiance, Anna found herself succumbing to the bleak realm of substance dependence and reckless sexual behavior. The profound alteration, specifically the morally promiscuous conduct, caused immense distress to those in her vicinity, as Anna was initially known for her reticence and introspective nature from a tender age. Suddenly, she began associating with unsavory individuals and seldom returned to her place of residence. Tara observed the unfolding events with an unexpected air of composure and apathy.

Fortunately, Anna did not incur any permanent harm during her eventful weekend of oblivion. Anna encountered individuals who exhibited pronounced tendencies towards social isolation and moral depravity. Given this, it is truly remarkable that Anna was able to extricate herself from that milieu relatively unscathed. Nevertheless, the dysfunctional dynamic between her and her mother endured. Presently, her mother cohabits with her new husband, who similarly exhibits minimal concern for his Step-daughter's misfortune. Therefore, the couple resides in their own residence while providing assistance to Anna for her self-sustaining lifestyle. Furthermore, this serves as an additional indication of a mother exhibiting narcissistic traits. Tara presently finds it highly advantageous to fully relinquish her previous lifestyle and center her attention solely on the novel aspect she possesses - her recent marriage. It is comparatively more convenient for her to remit funds on a monthly basis to Anna instead of actively assisting her. Anna resides in solitude, exhibiting limited capacity to independently attend to her personal well-being, burdened by a multitude of uncertainties and unresolved matters that trouble her on a daily basis.

Anna was diagnosed with a borderline personality disorder an extended period ago. We have previously acknowledged that the origins of both narcissistic and borderline personality disorders emanate from a shared root cause - suboptimal parental approaches and inherent genetic susceptibility. Despite their apparent dissimilarity and lack of connection in their extreme manifestations, these two disorders exhibit remarkable parallels. The convergence of their paths pertains to a subject matter that we have extensively expounded upon in other contexts - individuals who exhibit characteristics of vulnerable narcissism. Firstly, vulnerable narcissists exhibit the same grandiose sense of self that is distinctive of their stable counterparts. In contrast, vulnerable narcissists exhibit instability and suffer from profound inner insecurity and a dearth of self-assurance, which indeed constitutes the defining attribute of individuals with borderline personalities.

Certain psychoanalysts posit that a regression towards the borderline personality structure is a phenomenon that occurs in virtually all individuals, albeit in a more regulated and implicit manner. Owing to their proximity to the borderline register, narcissists, particularly those who are vulnerable, tend to exhibit a tendency towards regressing into a less stable configuration reminiscent of borderline characteristics. It is conceivable to postulate that Anna is highly likely to possess a borderline personality disorder, as her early identification with her mother has led to the internalization of certain narcissistic characteristics. Similar to how narcissism is not without borderline characteristics, the borderline condition is not without narcissistic traits.

In conclusion, it is imperative to shift our focus away from the ceaseless diagnosis and superfluous expressions of sympathy towards Anna. Instead, we must direct our attention towards facilitating her personal growth, enabling her to overcome the traumas that have plagued her existence.

Regrettably, a straightforward solution is not readily available. Similar to individuals with any type of personality disorder, her personality and character exhibit significant malformation. It does not resemble acquiring a flu-like illness, where one contracts it, experiences a brief period of coughing and discomfort, and subsequently begins to feel better. Regarding personality disorders, the intricacies involved are of a more intricate nature. It can be likened to possessing an inherently flawed immune system, wherein one becomes significantly more prone to overreacting, engaging in impulsive behavior, or cultivating maladaptive emotional reactions in the face of seemingly inconsequential life occurrences. To clarify, a personality disorder can be characterized as an enduring and profound susceptibility that extends across various aspects of an individual's life.

It is likely evident to you at this point how challenging it can be to manage individuals with personality disorders. There exists a distinct category of therapists who have acquired expertise in addressing such cases, as the process of recovery demands considerable dedication, endurance, and diligent effort from both the individual seeking treatment and the therapist. For instance, Anna initiated various therapeutic sessions on multiple occasions. Nevertheless, on each occasion, adverse outcomes occurred - whether it be the therapist's perceived attempt to engage in inappropriate behavior, or their unfeeling and apathetic attitude. On other occasions, all would appear to transpire favorably, only to be followed by her disruptive and attention-seeking behavior during therapy sessions. A noteworthy example of this occurred when the therapist endeavored to communicate to her about her occasional tendencies towards narcissism and egotism. This provided a sufficient pretext for her to exhibit a furious response and completely discontinue psychotherapy.

Hence, there exists a cohort of therapists whose primary focus is on providing assistance to individuals afflicted with personality disorders. Initially, they are well aware that the management of these individuals will not be characterized by expeditiousness and brevity. They are aware that effective treatment protocols may extend over a duration of 2 to 3 years, and in some cases, continue throughout one's lifetime. Furthermore, they are poised to witness the disintegration of their commendable efforts due to a single impulsive decision made by their clientele. For instance, Anna had the fortuity of discovering a skilled therapist, with whom she cultivated a robust and deeply empathetic rapport. Everything appeared to be going smoothly until Anna made the choice to make a final visit to a club where she used to engage in hedonistic activities fueled by drugs in the past. It is unnecessary to mention that the duration of the aforementioned "last time" persisted for several days, following which it appeared as if numerous months of diligent labor had been rendered futile. At the very moment when circumstances appeared to be favorable, Anna committed a regrettable action, necessitating her to recommence the entire process anew. At this juncture, a significant number of therapists tend to relinquish their efforts. And they cannot be entirely held responsible; we must acknowledge that witnessing months of diligent effort being entirely negated by a single irrational act is undeniably challenging.

Metallization-Based Therapy

Fortunately, practitioners adhering to Fonagy's therapeutic framework, commonly known as Mentalization Based Therapy, possess a deep understanding of this phenomenon and exhibit composure even in the face of their clients' impulsive behaviors. In situations of this nature, the paramount consideration is for the patient to acknowledge the presence of unwavering support from another individual, irrespective of the circumstances.

To begin with, mentalization-based treatment takes considerable influence from psychoanalysis, but it also heavily incorporates contemporary therapeutic approaches such as cognitive-behavioral and integrative therapies. The concept of mentalization has its origins in the theoretical framework of the Kleinian school of thinking.

The authors of the Handbook put forth the contention that there exist various categories of patients. Initially, an illustration of an individual greatly affected by trauma was presented - specifically, a person who experienced childhood sexual abuse but managed to effectively suppress this extremely distressing recollection. However, during a particularly demanding period in his life, the unwelcome recollections resurfaced. During this period of heightened stress, an individual, referred to as Steven for the purpose of this discussion, sought therapy. And what ultimately proved to be most beneficial for him was to revisit and vividly recall the distressing event. Due to his tender age at the time of experiencing sexual abuse, he was unable to engage in rational reflection on the matter. This aspect of his character remained submerged within the depths of his psyche throughout his life, shrouded in darkness and untouched by his conscious awareness. In this rudimentary form, the trauma cannot be cured. Therefore, the therapist advocated for him to engage in open discussions regarding his traumatic experiences and, if feasible, to revisit those experiences in a controlled manner while maintaining a state of tranquility and self-possession. This had a significantly favorable impact on his disposition.

Cultivate Reciprocal Relationships

Inquire for assistance Seek guidance Request support Solicit aid

You are not solitary, and there exists a multitude of individuals who have encountered or are presently undergoing similar circumstances. Do not hesitate to seek assistance and establish a network of support that can provide you with the necessary resources to maintain equilibrium, stability, and unwavering self-assurance in your decisions and ongoing path.

It is not attributable to any fault on your part that the individual with whom you are in a relationship fails to comprehend their disorder or issue. Moreover, even if you were previously capable of perpetuating it by facilitating their behavior for an extended duration, rest assured that you possess the ability to recover and acquire the skills necessary to break free from such repeated patterns.

Assistance is readily accessible and pervasive in your surroundings. If access to a public support group is unavailable or if one does not feel at ease discussing the matter with friends and family, they should consider utilizing online platforms to explore additional sources of support and information. Explore opportunities to become a member of an undisclosed organization if you wish to safeguard your anonymity. Inquire of others about their experiences and the progress they have made in their recuperation. By actively seeking assistance and allowing it to alleviate the concerns that you may bear any responsibility for your encounter, you will acquire a wealth of knowledge and insight.

The key to moving on from a narcissistic relationship lies in cultivating a sense of mindfulness and fortitude. Granting yourself the capacity to derive greater satisfaction from life by fostering an equitable alliance is an entitlement that all individuals merit, and you are making commendable progress towards attaining that objective. Mitigate the repetitive nature of these patterns by cultivating self-compassion, maintaining an introspective approach to your personal growth, consistently addressing your emotions, choosing the morally upright path, familiarizing yourself with indicators of narcissistic behavior, and promptly seeking assistance whenever you require guidance.

You are making significant progress towards becoming the self-assured, content, and harmonious individual that you have always recognized and aspired to be. Acquiring the skills to navigate the narcissistic relationship may initially appear challenging, but rest assured that you possess all necessary resources to acknowledge your experiences and embark upon the path towards healing.

Engaging in an imbalanced relationship where one party solely prioritizes their own needs is morally incorrect. This type of relationship invariably yields unfavorable outcomes, making it advisable to consult a professional who can provide guidance for navigating such circumstances. In the majority of instances, one's ability to effectively handle individuals of this nature tends to be limited, as they commonly exhibit signs of excessive possessiveness. They employ manipulative tactics to compel you to remain in a dysfunctional relationship, as they perceive you as belonging to them. Moreover, they consistently manage to attribute any flaws within the relationship to your actions, leaving you burdened with the blame. They exhibit exceptional skill in deflecting responsibility onto the more vulnerable individual within the relationship. They manipulate your emotions and leverage them as a means to exploit you. Consequently, in the majority of instances, one experiences a sense of confinement akin to imprisonment. You will be emotionally blackmailed into not seeing walking away as an option.

However, a qualified practitioner in the field of mental health will assist you in effectively addressing the dynamics within the relationship. Occasionally, moving on may not offer a suitable resolution; one alternative is to pursue a treatment centered on fostering dependency in a constructive manner, enabling you to maintain the relationship while promoting overall well-being. The principle underlying pro-dependence is to carefully deliberate upon the benefits of coexisting with individuals who push our boundaries, and to shift our attention towards the advantages that we gain from them, rather than dwelling on any negative aspects or dreading potential hardships that could stem from such interactions. We could greatly derive advantages from their strengths. Additionally, they have the potential to benefit from our contributions. In actuality, it is possible to establish a mutually beneficial dynamic within the relationship, where both individuals derive advantages from one another.

Arguably, the most effective approach for managing the repercussions of terminating a relationship with a narcissist is to seek out a reputable support network. There are numerous online and offline communities that one can join with the specific purpose of exploring narratives from individuals who have encountered comparable experiences to their own.

Identifying individuals who have encountered narcissists in their lives can facilitate a deeper comprehension that you were never at fault, while acknowledging the presence of such individuals within our society. The more promptly you come to comprehend the verity that narcissists bear responsibility for their own unsuccessful relationships, the more promptly you can absolve yourself for permitting the abuse to transpire.

Similarly, it would be beneficial for you to seek someone who can offer profound understanding into your distinct emotions. Therapists who possess a deep understanding of narcissistic abuse can assist you in comprehending and revealing the underlying truths regarding the actions exhibited by your narcissistic abuser. These individuals can additionally impart to you invaluable coping strategies and activities that can expedite and enhance the process of healing.

No contact

During the initial phase following the termination of your relationship, whether it lasts for a few days or weeks, you may experience a persistent inclination to reintegrate and express remorse. In accordance with a common pattern observed in those who perceive themselves as victims, it is likely that you are experiencing a profound sense of wrongdoing, prompting you to believe that it is necessary for you to extend an apology for your behavior.

At this juncture, it is imperative that you recollect the reasons that impelled your departure initially. Revisit the instances of mistreatment and gain a broader understanding of the situation. Reflect upon the anguish, the desertion, the censure, and the depreciation and recognize that these were authentic encounters that brought you considerable discomfort.

Refrain from assigning blame to yourself and uphold strict avoidance of any form of communication or interaction with your abuser. Allow yourself the necessary duration to undergo a healing process and to perceive matters with an unobscured perspective, rather than the distorted lens imposed upon you by the manipulative individual. If it is necessary, you might want to consider taking a temporary respite from social media and keeping your mobile device at a distance from you. Engage in a meaningful pursuit or cultivate a pastime to occupy your thoughts and prevent dwelling on the actions of your narcissistic abuser.

Is it invariably appropriate to disengage from a narcissistic individual?

Refusing the advances of an individual with narcissistic tendencies, be it in actuality or from their perspective, is prone to incurring intense emotional distress or indignation within them, as it inflicts a profound wound to their narcissistic self-image. A spurned romantic partner may experience profound anguish when the object of their love no longer reciprocates their affections. Similarly, a narcissist experiences profound grievance when a provider of narcissistic validation - or anyone else, for that matter - determines that they do not meet the standard of being "sufficiently excellent."

Individuals with profound narcissism, exhibiting an exceptionally heightened state of vigilance, might perceive feelings of rejection due to factors that would not typically affect individuals of average disposition. Rejecting their request for your company or collaboration due to a busy schedule or insufficient rationale may inadvertently trigger a strong and unanticipated reaction. It is optimal to provide them with a justified reason that lies outside of your influence rather than demonstrating a voluntary refusal. When it comes to being unable to meet or see someone, it is advisable to have comprehensively valid reasons, such as having work commitments that extend into the late hours due to a crucial deadline, being obligated to attend a significant wedding, or being already scheduled for a vacation or trip in another location.

Narcissists have a strong aversion to losing.

They really don't. "When you assert that your relationship has terminated, it is a sincere declaration, yet the individual with narcissistic tendencies perceives it as an overt provocation, an opportunity to intensify their narcissistic behavior and interpret it as a formidable challenge.

Narcissists Pursue Victory

Despite appearances, he or she will not actively pursue you. No, conversely, their intention is to restore the status quo, wherein they retain complete authority and you acquiesce to their mistreatment, all while showering them with unwavering devotion and admiration. Please be assured that if you choose to yield and return, there will undoubtedly be consequences for your decision to abandon. The individual in question indeed desires your return, although it is contingent upon meeting their specific conditions and exhibiting identical or potentially heightened levels of self-centeredness and narcissistic tendencies present at the time of your departure – the very reasons behind your departure.

Narcissistic individuals have a desire to frequently monitor your activities.

Is it possible that this individual's affections towards you endure? Not likely. It must be acknowledged that it is highly probable that they never truly harbored genuine feelings of love towards you. Their sole objective is to ensure your enduring sorrow, perpetual unhappiness, and reliance on their presence for any semblance of contentment. For a narcissist, the gratification lies in the awareness that your profound unhappiness and distress in their absence are equally fulfilling, if not more so, compared to successfully luring you back into their company.

Ultimately, if one's partner fails to consistently captivate their focus throughout the course of the relationship, it is expected that they will desire confirmation of their constant presence in one's thoughts and encounter difficulty in their absence. Eventually, the individual will extend an offer to alleviate distress by graciously accepting your apology and reinstating your connection. This substantial error will inevitably lead to a recurrence of abuse once you revert to their authority, perpetuating an unceasing cycle. The ultimate source of gratification for a narcissist lies in manipulating your emotions, causing you to vacillate between remaining in their presence and departing. This delicate dance bestows upon the narcissist an unparalleled sense of power and dominance over you.

How to Depart

Provided that you remain ensnared by the influence of a narcissistic individual, your ability to progress effectively will continue to be hindered. It is imperative that you disassociate from individuals before you can make progress in any endeavor.

Nevertheless, given the extensive duration of your relationship and the potential existence of shared parental responsibilities, extracting oneself from such a partnership may prove arduous.

Nevertheless, employing the appropriate strategies will enable you to depart from the individual with desired outcomes.

Presented below are several recommendations to assist you in safely extricating yourself from an abusive relationship.

Do not afford them the final opportunity.

Upon separation from an abusive narcissistic individual, their subsequent behavior typically involves employing seduction tactics in an attempt to entice your return, only to subsequently discard you once the objective is achieved. The primary objective of a narcissist is to ensure that you are consistently held accountable for any and all circumstances.

They desire complete control over all aspects, and when situations do not align with their preferences, they ingeniously manage to shift the dynamics in their favor. In the event that the narcissist is not prepared for departure, they will employ persuasive tactics and beseech you fervently, imploring and expressing remorse."

To ensure your departure, endeavor to prevent them from exerting control over you once more. They will initiate the act of beseeching and subsequently engage in fervently pleading with you, expressing remorse and earnestly imploring your return.

Refrain from disclosing your departure

There is no necessity to communicate your decision to discontinue the relationship with the narcissist. This is due to the possibility that they may engage in love bombing behavior in order to ensnare you within the confines of the relationship. They may resort to the extreme measure of threatening self-harm in order to manipulate you into remaining, thereby constraining your freedom of choice.

Possess Excess Funds

When contemplating your departure, it is crucial to ascertain that you possess sufficient financial resources to facilitate a smooth transition into your new existence. Commence early financial planning in order to ensure that once the opportune moment arises for your departure, you won't find yourself compelled to return to someone for the assistance they provide.

If your partner exhibits abusive behavior, it is crucial to undertake all necessary measures discreetly to avoid being completely ostracized by said individual.

Submit an Official Complaint Regarding the Act of Misconduct

You may not currently possess the appropriate standing to escalate the matter to the police; however, it is imperative that you formally document the occurrence of abuse. Upon entering, it is imperative that you articulate the events that have transpired and, if present, visually demonstrate any discernible injuries.

When you document a declaration, you will possess a record that can be cited when you choose to present a legal argument at a subsequent point in time.

Sign out from all devices

If you persist in remaining logged into devices distributed among your associates, it is imperative to alter the passwords of said devices to prevent your activities from being monitored by said associates. Perform a comprehensive reset of all credentials and generate fresh authentication information.

Hence, kindly compile an exhaustive inventory of all the platforms you have previously accessed, the instances you have utilized your credit card for transactions, and any instances in which you have enabled autofill. Subsequently, swiftly proceed to eliminate said records in their entirety.

Upon disconnection from the devices, it is imperative to ensure that one is not subject to any form of surveillance or tracking. If feasible, kindly dispose of the phone and procure a replacement device that can be utilized.

Do not allow yourself to be influenced by compliments.

A narcissist will endeavor to employ flattery or any other tactic to impede your departure. The objective is to establish an atmosphere wherein you feel compelled to depart without alternative options.

The narcissist will endeavor to surpass your expectations by employing a range of tactics, such as showering you with lavish gifts and lavishing upon you the attention you have long yearned for.

Reestablish Connections with Loved Ones

An individual exhibiting narcissistic and abusive behavior will seek to isolate you from your familial relationships while asserting their claim to their undivided attention. It is possible that you have not maintained relationships with individuals who were once important to you, and perhaps you have inadvertently disregarded their presence. However, the paramount objective is for you to establish a renewed connection with them, thereby enlisting their aid in facilitating your recovery.

Notwithstanding, it is imperative for you to cease experiencing shyness and embarrassment in their presence. If it becomes necessary to express remorse, then one should suppress one's ego and extend an apology.

Upon reestablishing contact with them, you will come to discern the extent of the individuals' concerted efforts to assist you, albeit without achieving the desired outcomes. It is possible that they attempted to provide assistance, but they were inexperienced and uncertain about how to initiate the process.

Thoroughly sanitize the ship's surfaces

Now is an opportune moment to ascertain individuals who may be detrimental to your objectives and subsequently separate oneself from them. You will render a decision, yet it is not reasonable to anticipate universal understanding from all parties involved. They will cast blame upon you and feign superiority as if they are unparalleled in the world.

You should consider this as an opportune moment to disassociate yourself from certain individuals in your circle, particularly those who pose a hindrance to the realization of your objectives.

Strategies for navigating a complex relationship with the presence of children

Interacting with individuals who display narcissistic tendencies can prove to be arduous, exhausting, and occasionally, truly distressing, especially when there is no personal benefit derived from such encounters. It is even worse when there are children involved. You may initiate the process by examining whether there exist any realms in which you could alter your perspective. Whilst you may harbor aversion towards the notion of self-transformation, particularly when it is incumbent upon the individual possessing narcissistic tendencies to initiate such change, it nevertheless presents a promising avenue for embarking upon this journey.

There are individuals who have already experienced parenthood and, are inclined to provide their children with the opportunity of being nurtured by both parents without any deprivation. However, some individuals mention financial motives as a rationale; despite his narcissistic tendencies, he is fulfilling his financial obligations.

Opting to remain presents itself as a legitimate decision. You have the ability to assume command of the relationship and guarantee that you do not endure any undue hardship in the course of it.

Establish limits

This constitutes the initial measure to ensure that your partner does not exploit your vulnerabilities. Please compile a comprehensive inventory of the matters that you deem unacceptable and will not tolerate. This could encompass behaviors such as engaging in derogatory language, delivering critical remarks, issuing threats, raising one's voice, spreading falsehoods, exerting pressure, among other actions. It is crucial to document them as evidence.

There should be repercussions for violating established boundaries. If you have communicated to your partner that should he engage in shouting, you intend to disengage and retire to the designated guest bedroom, it is advisable to follow through with this course of action. He will make attempts to exert influence over you in an effort to weaken your determination. Should you choose to proceed in such manner, it will be apparent to him that he can act with impunity. He will persistently challenge the limits, and before long, you will find yourself in the same initial position once again.

Did his behavior undergo any modifications upon your establishment of boundaries? It may be in your best interest to exert influence over the manner in which he communicates with you, as this could potentially lead to his deliberate avoidance of any communication with you. He employs a tactic of silence towards you. This demonstrates a lack of awareness or disregard for established limits. Don't worry. He doesn't need to. He merely needs to acknowledge their significance for the benefit of your relationship.

Initiate discussions of this nature when he is in a favorable disposition. He is more inclined to lend an ear in that case.

Please pay attention/heed to what I am about to say.

Narcissists are often afforded minimal attention by individuals. Once they begin to speak, individuals in their vicinity commence contemplating, 'oh, here we go again with their lofty discourse.' Consequently, they disengage mentally. And one can scarcely assign fault to them. Engaging in self-aggrandizing discourse can be quite tiring, you know.

Take the opportunity to heed his words. Despite his potentially self-aggrandizing or victimizing tendencies, it would be wise to lend an ear to his words. He will perceive your sincere concern for his well-being, consequently fostering an improved treatment towards you.

Please remain composed.

How you behave in times of conflict goes a long way in determining the nature of your relationship with a narcissist. He will attempt to elicit a response from you in order to satisfy his belief that he wields influence over your emotional state. Your capacity to maintain a composed demeanor deprives him of that authority.

In the event that the situation appears to be escalating beyond control, it would be advisable to jointly pursue assistance. Receiving objective feedback on the impact of his actions may stimulate introspection within him, ultimately leading to a proactive approach in seeking personal transformation.

Obsessive Creatures

Regardless of how much they feign an intense interest in you or anyone else, it is essential to recognize that their motivations extend beyond a genuine admiration for you or anyone they believe to be outstanding.

Their objective is to create a state of complete dependence on their attention. To engender a profound adoration in others. The sole remarkable individual in the realm of a Narcissistic person is none other than themselves. The significance of individuals is disregarded unless they can be utilized or leveraged for personal benefits or satisfaction.

They live for self-idolization. Their typical ability to attain their desires, which forms the foundation of their self-justification, may lead them to perceive themselves as the privileged superior figures.

Throughout their lives, they consistently managed to evade the negative personal consequences of their actions by employing a combination of manipulation, deception, and intimidation, without displaying any remorse or reflection whatsoever. Sacrificing any necessary individuals in the pursuit of their goals.

The emphasis lies in their image.

Their actual state holds negligible importance to them; it is solely the perception of others that holds significance. How they look to the outside world therefore and what they manage to procure for themselves as a consequence.

Having a comprehensive understanding of one's adversary significantly increases the likelihood of achieving victory in the conflict. Similar to handling a venomous serpent. You are aware of its toxicity, whereas you possess immunity.

Furthermore, it is common knowledge that rendering the poison ineffective can be achieved by employing a spade to sever its head and subsequently interring it. In addition, it is essential to exercise caution and maintain a safe distance from the snake to avoid its potential to strike.

This implies that by effectively employing factual information, one has the potential to achieve victory. How does this relate?

It is commonly understood that individuals with Narcissistic traits exhibit cunning and manipulative tendencies, capitalizing on favorable circumstances to act in a similar manner to a serpent.

You are also cognizant of this fact, thus employ this knowledge precisely to your benefit.

Maintain a suitable distance while ensuring constant vigilance towards them.

Similar to an extensive array of venomous species, opting to run is an exceptionally poor decision.

It is imperative to maintain a constant state of awareness regarding their persistent need for victory, unwavering desire to be correct, and insistence on having things conform to their personal preferences.

In the event that this does not come to fruition, their demeanor becomes disagreeable, somber, or resentful, or they fall ill as per their request.

The dominant authority in their realm abides by the principle of granting their desires. This holds utmost preoccupation for them.

They will assert to individuals that they possess exceptional social aptitude, yet in reality, their main proficiency lies in their remarkable manipulation skills.

Why it is Hard to Let go

Narcissistic individuals forge a formidable connection with whomever assumes the role of their partner. And it can present difficulties in terms of dissolution. Empirical evidence has demonstrated that achieving ultimate success typically requires more than a mere two to three attempts. However, there is no need for concern as you need not engage in repetitive actions prior to emancipation. Here are the reasons why it is challenging, and once you grasp that concept, you will liberate yourself from their constraints.

1. A Narcissistic individual emulates your mannerisms and behaviors in order to mold themselves into an idealized version of your romantic partner. During the initial phase of the romantic connection, a Narcissist would exhibit a keen interest in acquiring extensive knowledge about your person. He initiates the process by familiarizing himself with your preferences and subsequently reflects them onto his own actions. Consequently, he has the ability to create a psychological milieu that will facilitate the formation of a profound and secure attachment on your part. They employ an excessive amount of flattery and frequently offer reassurance that they will address your most profound insecurities. Their main objective is simply to lull you into complacency, thus rendering you

susceptible to their influence. Thus, you possess an unwavering allegiance to them that cannot be diminished.

2. They are oblivious to the imminent conclusion of the relationship. A person exhibiting narcissistic traits may perceive the relationship to be in a temporary state of suspension if their attention is directed towards someone else or if they are experiencing anger. However, they consistently terminate the relationship with you. Therefore, according to their sentiment, they maintain that you are their rightful possession, from which you are unlikely to depart. They possess the authority to determine the commencement and termination of their relationships. They consistently endeavor to ensure that you violate any non-communication strategy you are devising.

3. You are inundated with inquiries. Undoubtedly, there will be numerous facets within the relationship that may elude your comprehension. You may

begin to inquire about his genuine feelings for you, and as you attempt to unravel these uncertainties, you find yourself fixated on the dynamics of the relationship rather than summoning the courage to terminate it. Instead of taking decisive action and asserting your own worth, you convince yourself that things will improve and that all your lingering questions will be answered, causing further delay and perpetuating the belief that relief can only come with a response.

4. You cultivate a chemical connection with him. The connection that is present between you and the narcissist is a result of a chemical interaction. Where it oscillated between kindness and malevolence. And as a result, you may begin experiencing withdrawal symptoms and developing a dependence, which was initially beyond your control. This addictive behavior has the potential to hinder the progression of your life and impede your ability to disengage.

5. You have developed a strong emotional attachment to him based on shared experiences of trauma. These bonds exhibit remarkable parallels with Stockholm Syndrome. In this particular form of interpersonal connection, you undergo a process of psychological manipulation that instills within you a sense of unwavering allegiance towards him. And what is the cause for this occurrence? The kindness shown to you, intended to alleviate your suffering, is solely responsible for the allowances you have been granted. And thus, you are compelled to adhere to the notion that every transgression will invariably culminate in benevolence. Hence, the provisional comprehension he imparts shall inadvertently be misconstrued as sincere concern, ultimately ensnaring you in a state of anticipation for a future that shall never materialize.

6. You've Been Gaslighted. Narcissistic individuals commonly employ gaslighting tactics, causing individuals to

experience doubt and uncertainty regarding their own reality. And subsequently, you cease to place reliance on your instinct. You cease to have faith in your own discernment, and a sense of doubt sets in, questioning the accuracy of your emotions. You commence to encounter challenges in comprehending the inherent qualities or merits within you. Consequently, you place your trust in his discernment rather than your own. You observe his presence before you, and you do not perceive yourself as deserving of blame. You lean towards remaining in the relationship under the belief that he is concealing your errors, and departing would risk exposing your inadequate conduct.

7. You hold yourself accountable for the difficulties encountered within the relationship. When it comes to verbal and mental games of twisting and changing games, he is an expert. He engages in discussions where he is aware of his own fallibility in order to opportunistically redirect the blame

onto you. Frequently, one's perception often entails recurring instances of envy, oppressive behavior, and derogatory language. However, your cognitive faculties will perceive it as an unintended incident rather than an actual event.

8. You perceive a sense of isolation from the ample support available for your selection. Your narcissistic partner has the potential to sever ties that could aid in your reawakening. Those acquaintances who will inquire about the reasons for your continued involvement, companions who will assert that you bear responsibility for maintaining the connection, individuals who will assist in fostering a discerning mindset. Irrespective of the matter at hand, you may experience a sense of lacking in terms of having a readily available support system to rely upon during moments of distress. Is it indeed the case that you lack such a support system? Not really. Your physical distance from them coupled with your

spouse's behavior resembling that of a narcissist suggests that you are detached from their actions.

9. You consistently discern the positive attributes within him. Indubitably, consistently fixating on an individual's shortcomings is detrimental to one's well-being. However, for what duration ought you to persist in assuming complete responsibility? What is the recommended duration for enduring such a barrage of insults? Instead of employing such a line of reasoning. You are persuading yourself that he is engaging in that action involuntarily. It is certain that you will come to the belief that he harbors benevolent intentions. You possess a remarkable capacity for forgiveness, yet within the depths of your being, you grapple with an internal struggle against a persistent tormentor, yearning for the day when it shall cease.

10. You Desire a Formal Termination of the Relationship. Indeed, it will not advance. Why? You already know. The

narcissist exhibits a disinclination for being informed about your decision to sever ties; when such information is conveyed, they become incensed and agitated. This evokes contemplation regarding his desire for the relationship. He will proceed to strongly request that you remain. Your likelihood of remaining for an extended period is greater if you possess the intention to terminate the relationship in a manner consistent with a conventional breakup. The most effective approach would be to initiate an unplanned separation, wherein you gradually create emotional and physical distance between yourself and him, without prior notification.

How To Cope With The Challenges You Have Encountered

You have contemplated the emotions you will experience as you progress beyond the stage of healing, and you have discerned the challenges inherent in extricating oneself from a relationship with a Narcissist. However, one must contemplate the means by which they can ultimately regain control over their life. It requires a significant amount of time and one should not anticipate the swift disappearance of this countenance. Due to the involvement of your cognitive and physiological faculties. They are compelled to engage in their survival mechanism. They are required to acquire knowledge of a novel pattern and supplant the previous model that was once in place.

The crucial notion that can aid you in achieving this objective is the capacity to disengage oneself emotionally. This is the method by which one acquires the ability to differentiate between what rightfully belongs to them and what does not, undertaking this discernment not propelled by fear but driven instead by genuine affection for one's own existence and consciousness.

You are required to effectively regulate your internal thoughts, physical sensations, and dreams. Engaging in this endeavor will facilitate your personal expansion and recuperation, ultimately resulting in a profound metamorphosis. Engaging in this endeavor is the sole course of action that can ensure establishment of a genuine connection with oneself, facilitate a well-informed decision-making process, and enable the envisioning of a more promising future. Outlined below are seven pragmatic approaches to reclaiming control over your life and embodying your desired self.

1. Do not perceive the narcissist as a human being. Now is not the appropriate

moment to dwell upon the narcissist. This is an opportune moment to begin considering one's own well-being, a notion that runs counter to the desires of an individual with narcissistic tendencies. They express a wish for you to become engrossed in comprehending their nature, thereby leading to the introduction of ambiguity. Consequently, you develop a misaligned perception of yourself and your emotions. Initially, upon the advent of contemplation, it is essential to reaffirm to oneself that it is an ensnarement and acknowledge that one's initial intuition was correct in relinquishing its hold. One may list their desired qualities in a relationship and mark them off as they observe if any are reciprocated. It is probable that none will be returned, which indicates the correctness and fairness of one's decision. Therefore, partake of actuality.

2. Release your emotions to allow a narcissist to have power over you. Currently, it is not an opportune moment for you to embark on

elucidating the various ways in which the narcissist has caused harm to you. Please recall that you have previously taken this action prior to arriving at your current determination. There is no purpose in attempting to resume this matter. Continual elucidation on your part nurtures their cravings and engenders a feeling of fulfillment in them. They perceive themselves as ultimately undermining your authority. In doing so, you have the potential to inflict harm upon them through your failure to effectively articulate your emotions and rationale for not desiring to reestablish a relationship with them. When they request clarification, and you refrain from providing it, you undermine their self-esteem and elicit distress. Rather than implying that your actions were incorrect, they are prompted to reflect on the strategies they employed incorrectly.

3. Swiftly Establish a Circular Perimeter Around Your Person. The longer you ruminate on past events, the greater the

likelihood of experiencing remorse and encountering negative consequences. In order to extricate yourself from this predicament, promptly venture beyond the confines of your comfort zone and cultivate companionship with individuals of affinity. If feasible, undertake lengthy journeys to seek out an acquaintance from yesteryears who shall serve as an emblematic representation of genuine affection, thus reaffirming your understanding of veritable love. Participate in a community initiative that centers on the process of recovering from a traumatic relationship. Additionally, should you have any preferred games in mind, do not hesitate to invite your friends for a collective play session. It is imperative that the material you engage with holds significant importance. Therefore, peruse a literary work that primarily expounds on the cultivation of one's resilience. You may choose to peruse a multitude of literary works that expound upon the given topic.

4. Cut Off Contacts. It is important to remember that an individual demonstrating narcissistic traits may strive to retaliate against you and seek to make you reevaluate the relationship. By keeping them within your thoughts and maintaining the ability to observe and engage with them once more, you can effectively navigate this situation. Thus, if you possess their contact information, kindly eliminate it. Similarly, if they are connected with you on any of your social media platforms, please remove them from your network. You do not possess sadistic tendencies; rather, you exhibit a realistic perspective.

However, what if the individual in question happens to be a colleague within one's professional environment? You shall continue to interact with them, but how might you effectively uphold a firm boundary in doing so? And ensure that you are fully persuaded that the limit you establish is indeed correct. They might perceive it as being severe, choose to disregard it, as you are not obligated to provide anyone - not even the narcissist, with an elucidation regarding your lifestyle choices. If they are your parents, chances are that as an adult, you may no longer rely on residing with them, taking heed of their counsel, but rather prioritize following your own convictions.

5. Demand For Balance. And from who? Regarding your own well-being, it is highly probable that one may experience a sense of imbalance, which can be remedied by engaging in actions that are antithetical to those of the narcissist. Instead of indulging in self-criticism stemming from your past experiences, choose to embrace self-awareness. And frequently acknowledge the positive aspects within oneself. Take the time to decelerate and devote your complete attention to enhancing the caliber of your life. Exceed your comfort zone. Thus, consistently strive to cultivate a genuine longing for greater acquisition. Dismiss any uncertainty; it does not

define your essence, as it is not reflective of your true self. Once again write the negative thoughts you were thrown at while in the relationship, then in front of it, write the strength. Reflect upon the attributes that are esteemed by certain individuals; make efforts to cultivate and enhance those attributes. As you engage in the active cultivation of these attributes. You will reduce your focus on the negative remarks that were directed towards you.

6. Abstain from seeking their approval. It is logically linked to the previous point that was discussed. This primarily holds true in cases where the individual displaying narcissistic traits occupies the role of a colleague. It is applicable to individuals who have infrequent encounters with their former partners.

Nevertheless, this does not imply that you are incapable of doing enjoyable things for them when the circumstances are appropriate. The sole admonition is to refrain from engaging in such actions solely to garner their favor. Furthermore, one should not anticipate receiving expressions of gratitude from them in the event that one carries out an act that pleases them. Should you anticipate acknowledgement, you will only inflict greater harm upon yourself, for it shall forever elude you. Previously, you were aware that their belief associates expressing gratitude solely with individuals of inferior character, rather than with those possessing superior intellect such as themselves.

Do not exert oneself excessively to accommodate their desires. And you will exacerbate your discomfort should you harbor the belief that you are poised to secure their favor. Indeed, I am quite confident that you have undoubtedly surpassed this developmental phase. Do not emulate their conduct; instead, embody the disposition of an emancipated individual who derives genuine gratification from their daily pursuits.

7. Help Others. One may understandably question how this situation can be reconciled given that assistance is also required. Nevertheless, it is important to acknowledge that providing assistance to others represents an additional pragmatic approach to attaining recovery from one's circumstances. Consider, do you have acquaintances who are presently endeavoring to regain their emotional well-being after enduring the anguish and assaults perpetrated by a Narcissist. Can you help them? Indeed, it is permissible for you to assume the role of their friend, with the objective of persuading them of their inherent worthiness and offering insight into the potential components of the recuperative phase. Additionally, it is imperative to instruct them that it is inappropriate to fixate on said matters. What are the intended outcomes of this action?

As you continue to relay the information, your growing conviction in having made the correct decision intensifies, eradicating any possibility of reversing course. In addition, there are further advantages. When you see that they are getting better, it convinces you that you are getting better too and you will get through finally. Therefore, by assisting them, you are concurrently aiding yourself in attaining an optimal degree of conviction.

8. Don't Pretend. There are occasions when one must acknowledge a sense of discomfort regarding the situation. Please refrain from feigning ignorance or denial regarding this matter, as it only exacerbates your emotional distress. In the event that such emotions arise, acknowledge their presence and devise a strategy to effectively relinquish such thoughts. Maintain a perpetual readiness to counteract negativity with positivity in every circumstance. There is no improvement beyond that. A person with narcissistic tendencies may endeavor to employ these tactics against you, leading you to internalize doubt in your judgment.

However, as one increasingly acknowledges the inevitability of such thoughts, one gains greater aptitude for effectively countering the associated emotions. Furthermore, refrain from indulging in the temptation to engage in verbal communication or engage in dialogue regarding your emotions with the individual exhibiting Narcissistic traits. It's disastrous. Do not allow him or her to broach the subject matter. Adhere to your principles and refrain from allowing his judgments to dictate your actions.

9. Always Trust Yourself. You may have experienced humiliation, condemnation, or social discomfiture as a consequence of voicing your viewpoint, and all of these circumstances can exert an impact on your psyche. And that generates a desire to establish a greater sense of affinity with them. However, the current reality is that it is imperative for you to cultivate self-confidence and reliance. Do not indulge in the notion of doubting

your own judgement. This could potentially deter you from undertaking risks. However, do not allow that to discourage you.

Prior to reaching a conclusion, ensure that you thoroughly validate your choice to ensure its optimal outcome. One can enhance the outcome of their decision-making process by embarking on comprehensive research prior to reaching a conclusion. In order to prevent the acquisition of a skewed perception of one's own self. You may have the opportunity to encounter individuals who possess greater knowledge than yourself and who will not boast about it. Instead, they will kindly guide and support you.

Assume accountability for your actions and acquire the skill of accepting responsibility for your endeavors, as this will clarify the distinction between instances where you are at fault and instances where you are not. The greater your realization, the stronger your self-trust grows in regard to your decision-making. Furthermore, it is evident that the decision you have made is leading you closer to achieving success. This will serve as additional motivation, reinforcing the fact that your departure from the toxic relationship is permanent and solely focused on your personal growth.

10. Find a Therapist. The significance of a therapist cannot be overemphasized. With their assistance, you have the ability to pursue the life you truly desire. A therapist will fulfill the dual role of being a counselor and a mentor. They monitor your progress. They possess an understanding of your emotions, having successfully navigated numerous circumstances, and are well versed in the strategies for reclaiming one's life. Please make sure to provide a comprehensive explanation of your thought process, including an evaluation of the likelihood and benefits, so that they have a clear understanding of the direction that needs to be taken.

Through the implementation of these ten effective strategies aimed at reclaiming your life, I can confidently guarantee that you will successfully become the individual you aspire to be. Indeed, it is possible for you to return to a state of being where you embody the highest and most optimal version of yourself.

During your early years, who established the precedent of consistently attributing blame to you? - Individuals who hold the perception that they are at fault for the dissolution of a romantic relationship often have a parent who unjustly placed an excessive amount of blame on them. The victim assumes a disproportionate amount of responsibility for a significant portion of the events that transpired within the relationship as a result of the aforementioned mistreatment endured during their formative years.

This aids in comprehending that a portion of what is veiling the present dissolution in a realistic manner is its resemblance to the cyclic childhood attribution scenario.

Why do you continue to defend the individual who is inflicting harm upon you? What are the benefits or advantages you gain from it? -In addition to habit, the victim tends to attribute blame to themselves. For the victim to achieve progress and distance themselves from the abusive situation, it is advantageous for them to acknowledge the motivations behind their inclination to shield their former abuser and take sole responsibility.

Certain individuals who have experienced trauma may possess the belief that assuming responsibility for the adverse circumstances would facilitate the improvement of their interpersonal bond. They possess memories of their initial emotional state upon initiating the relationship—specifically, sentiments of exceptionalism and self-assurance. Prior to this relationship, no other individual had the capability to evoke the same sentiment within them as their abuser did.

In the event that an individual who has suffered from abuse becomes cognizant of the fact that their perpetrator exhibits traits of a narcissistic abuser and comprehends that reverting the person or the relationship to its initial state is an improbable feat, they are more likely to embark on the path towards recuperation.

As an individual progresses through the healing journey, gaining a clearer perspective of the relationship unclouded by idealized notions, they are capable of composing an authentic affirmation to supersede the initial statements expressed during the early stages of their recovery.

The aforementioned statements encapsulate the victim's current psychological consensus on truth:

- The responsibility for the abusive behavior lies solely with my abuser. I cannot be held responsible. The individual who subjected me to abuse has a documented record of engaging in abusive behavior.

Regardless of my efforts, I could not alter the outcome of the relationship.

- Initially, my abuser exhibits favorable behavior towards the individual. This is the method they employ to entice the individual into developing an affinity towards them.

Eventually, once the novelty diminishes and a new target is ensnared, they will proceed to mistreat the newly introduced individual.

Numerous individuals of the opposite gender deem me to possess distinct qualities that make me alluring and noteworthy. They exhibit a conventional level of attraction towards me and do not assume a contrary demeanor from their outward presentation.

In the event that an individual who was previously victimized experiences a longing for their former abuser or falls back into self-blame, it is advisable for them to reacquaint themselves with the aforementioned statements (Greenberg, https://www.psychologytoday.com/us/blog/understanding-narcissism/201710/the-survival-guide-living-narcissist, 2017).

Severing familial ties

The process of disassociating from family members who exhibit narcissistic tendencies or align with the narcissist within your familial circle is inherently challenging.

It can be exceedingly difficult to create distance from your narcissistic parent(s) due to their significant influence in shaping your upbringing, past experiences, and overall trajectory, as they guided you into the world. The depth of the emotional connection you share with them might be somewhat compromised due to the presence of narcissistic tendencies within the relationship. Nonetheless, given their status as your parents, they will invariably occupy a significant role within your life and continue to maintain a place within your affections.

The act of distancing oneself from certain family members does not necessarily stem from their status as the narcissistic figures who inflicted abuse upon you. Your ex-partner, who exhibits narcissistic traits and has been abusive in the past, might persist in maintaining communication with your family members, potentially manipulating them into believing that you bear responsibility for the termination of the relationship. In the event that ongoing communication persists between your family and your former partner, it would be beneficial for your personal well-being and mental equilibrium to relinquish ties with both parties.

Irrespective of the causes for severing ties with relatives, it will present a significant challenge. Your absence may be noticed during family birthdays, holidays, weddings, and funerals. There is a possibility that certain family members may not be present at your personal occasions.

Your positive and negative memories will occasionally resurface in your thoughts. They will be bundled alongside diverse emotional states that may emerge and exert their influence upon you.

Isolation and Solitude

Narcissists exhibit a high degree of proficiency in the art of socially isolating their victims and strategically alienating significant individuals in order to establish and subsequently exert control over them. Narcissistic individuals who inflict abuse on their partners will make efforts to create distance between them and their family and friends, whereas narcissistic family members tend to exclude friends and potential romantic partners.

Upon liberating oneself from these relationships, one might find oneself confronted with a considerable amount of solitude during the initial stages. You may opt for solitude as you commence the process of reconstructing, rediscovering your identity, and recuperating from your encounter.

There can be instances when you desire to engage in social activities, yet your previous relationship may have jeopardized numerous valued friendships that were once reliable or strained bonds with close family members.

Attaining liberation can elicit both soothing and dispiriting emotions to an equal degree. This dynamic will persist in oscillating between one end and the other for a certain duration.

Wanting Revenge

One potential stage that individuals might experience during the process of recovery is the inclination to pursue vengeance and reparation towards their former abuser characterized by narcissistic tendencies. You may desire for them to experience the same degree of suffering and emotional turmoil that you endured while in the course of your relationship with them.

Indeed, this is a customary response as you have transitioned from a susceptible state into a state of anger. Irrespective of the tempting allure and gratifying emotions revenge may evoke, one must acknowledge that engaging in vengeance would essentially entail the resurfacing and exacerbation of past traumas. The evocation of distressing emotions and recollections will merely impede your progression towards emancipation from your previous life and interpersonal bond.

While it is understandable that your emotions may compel you to believe that your ex ought to face consequences, prioritizing your personal growth and detaching from previous emotional distress takes precedence.

Your Curiosity

Upon severing ties with a narcissist, the element of curiosity shall serve as an additional cause for the disarray of one's emotions. Despite the multitude of unfavorable encounters you have had, your sentiment towards this individual persists. It is advisable to ascertain the individuals they are associating with, the places they frequent, and their activities. In the current era of widespread social media usage, this phenomenon presents a convenient avenue for monitoring their activities and potentially becoming ensnared in the aforementioned situation.

Viewing images of this individual with narcissistic tendencies from your previous experiences has the potential to evoke a plethora of emotional reactions and internal conflicts that may hinder your endeavors towards self-restoration.

Individuals with narcissistic tendencies exhibit a profound lack of empathy, showing little genuine concern for the emotional well-being of others. They have the ability to move on relatively quickly. Possessing an understanding of their actions can result in emotional instability and impede progress.

www.ingramcontent.com/pod-product-compliance
Lightning Source LLC
Chambersburg PA
CBHW050406120526
44590CB00015B/1855